Mountain Masculinity

—————— • ——————

*The Life and Writing
of Nello "Tex" Vernon-Wood
in the Canadian Rockies
1906–1938*

Yellowhead Expedition, 1911 (Nello Vernon-Wood—second from left)

Mountain Masculinity

The Life and Writing
of Nello "Tex" Vernon-Wood
in the Canadian Rockies
1906–1938

EDITED AND INTRODUCED BY ANDREW GOW AND JULIE RAK

IN COLLABORATION WITH HARRY W. GOW AND JOHN R. GOW

AU PRESS

© 2008 Andrew Gow and Julie Rak for the introduction
All stories © estate of Nello Vernon-Wood

Published by AU Press, Athabasca University
1200, 10011 – 109 Street
Edmonton, AB T5J 3S8

Library and Archives Canada Cataloguing in Publication

Wood, Tex, 1882–1978
Mountain masculinity : the life and writing of Nello "Tex" Vernon-Wood in the Canadian
Rockies, 1906–1938 / edited and introduced by Andrew Gow and Julie Rak ; with Harry
W. Gow and John R. Gow. Includes bibliographical references.
ISBN 978-1-897425-02-2 Issued also in electronic format.

1. Vernon-Wood, Tex, 1882–1978. 2. Outdoor life–Rocky Mountains, Canadian (B.C.
and Alta.). 3. Frontier and pioneer life–Rocky Mountains, Canadian (B.C. and Alta.).
4. Rocky Mountains, Canadian (B.C. and Alta.)–In literature. 5. Canada, Western–
In literature. 6. Outdoor writers–Alberta–Biography. 7. Hunting guides–
Alberta–Biography. 8. Banff Region (Alta.)–Biography. I. Gow, Andrew Colin
II. Rak, Julie, 1966– III. Gow, Harry W. IV. Gow, John R. V. Title.

FC218.W66M68 2008   971.23'302092   C2008-902081-2

Printed and bound in Canada by AGMV Marquis
Cover and book design by Virginia Penny, Interpret Design Inc.

All images courtesy of the Whyte Museum of the Canadian Rockies (WMCR),
Banff, Alberta.

CONTENTS

ACKNOWLEDGEMENTS

———————— • ————————

The editors would like to thank Mrs. Christina Vernon-Wood of Grindrod, BC, for all her help and encouragement; Harry and John Gow for their written reminiscences of their grandfather (as included in Appendices A and B), and Diana (née Gow) and John Wood for their assistance and especially for providing copies of family photographs.

Allison Jones did much necessary supplemental spadework at the Archives of the Whyte Museum of the Canadian Rockies during the summer of 2006, when she was the beneficiary of a Roger S. Smith Research Studentship, supported by the Faculty of Arts, University of Alberta. Linda Bridges (History and Classics, University of Alberta) carefully retyped all Tex's stories from photocopies of originals also held at the Whyte; any errors in transcription are ours, not hers. The archivists at the Whyte Museum were most helpful and forthcoming.

———————— • ————————

Julie Rak would like to thank Andrew Gow for being such a wonderful collaborator and for asking her to participate in this project. She also thanks Paul Hjartarson and Candida Rifkind for their generous provision of scholarly advice. Most of all, Julie thanks Danielle Fuller because she makes ordinary life into something extraordinary, every day.

NATIONAL *SPORTSMAN*, FEBRUARY, 1938

FOREWORD

———————•———————

When you're in Banff and you feel like mingling with the quality folks you can stroll across the bridge at the end of Banff Avenue, up to the Banff Springs Hotel and in the bar overlooking the golf course order a cocktail, maybe a Negroni: equal parts gin, Campari, sweet vermouth, and a shred of orange peel, invented, the menu tells you, in 1922 in Florence at the Casoni Bar. You feel slightly decadent, but you tell yourself you have earned it after a hard day in the mountains, or that you will earn it by working harder the next day, though you feel with your Gortex and GPS that you have no link with the early explorers of these mountains.

Yet on your hike up Spray Avenue you will have passed the site of Tex Vernon-Wood's house at number 120, where he lived between 1930 and 1938 while writing these stories, and as you sip your cocktail you will, for the duration of your sojourn in the bar, be closer to Tex's clients than if you were out skinning a bear. There was no middle class in mountain travel in the early twentieth century. You were either a wrangler or you were wealthy.

Reading Tex's stories in context brings this home. The first thing that hits you when you open the bound volume of *The Sportsman* is an ad for Tiffany & Co. Jewelers, and facing it an ad for Marmon Straight 8 Motor Cars of Indianapolis. This is followed by Canada Dry, "The Champagne of Ginger Ales" and we are in the realm of champagne tastes: advertisements for private planes like the Lockheed Sirius, endorsed by Charles Lindbergh—or the Bellaca five-place amphibian, which gives you the "freedom of land, air, and water," enabling you to land anywhere to hunt or fish. See a tempting lake? Just set down your Bellaca and throw out a line. This is February 1930. The stock market has crashed and the Depression is starting but you would

1

never know it. There is a photo story on skiing in the Swiss Alps, another on deep-sea fishing in the Bahamas (get that swordfish!), and a feature on the National Motor Boat Show, with pictures of the "Consolidated 55-foot all-mahogany, double-cabin, twin-screw express cruiser. Two speedway 180 h.p. marine engines give a speed of 23 m.p.h." It is this mahogany cruiser that faces Tex's first story, "Fifth Avenue Pilgrims Amid the Goats."

In 1895 Georg Simmel, the father of sociology, was provoked by the building of a railway up the Eiger—one of the most fearsome peaks in the Alps—to write, "It is said that it is part of one's education to see the Alps, but not education alone for its twin sister is 'affluence'." He noted that the total number of climbers who had previously scaled the peak on their own could now be brought up in a single day, and though he said, "I disagree with that foolish romanticism which saw difficult routes, prehistoric food and hard beds as an irremovable part of the stimulus of the good old days of alpine travel," still "the increased accessibility of alpine travels does cause us to question the benefit our civilization draws from it..." A few years later, in his *Philosophy of Money,* he returned to this theme, arguing that our devotion to nature is not the result of our being in nature but rather the opposite: it is not the peasants herding sheep on the mountain slopes who sing the praises of a pastoral getaway; it is the city dwellers. And our longing comes from our distance from nature and the abstract existence that urban life, based on a money economy, has forced upon us. Ironically, the conditions of the alpine sojourn form a link between money and nature at the very same time that it separates them. It is only the possession of money that allows us to take flight into nature.[1]

At 50¢ an issue *The Sportsman* was expensive. In large format, with glossy pages and paintings commissioned for the covers (the February 1930 issue pictures a white-bearded gentleman in a brown suit being poled through a tropical swamp by his African servant), it offers Brooks Brothers clothing for polo, or B. Altman's "Tallyho" hunting attire for women but no ads for fishing rods, much less tents or boats. Tex's story "This Guiding Game" is sandwiched between an article on "The Real Romance of Steeplechasing" and "Wind and Rain on the Riviera;" later in the issue

1. Georg Simmel, *The Philosophy of Money,* trans. Tom Bottomore and David Frisby (London: Routledge & Kegan Paul, 1978), Georg Simmel, "The Alpine Journey," in *Simmel on Culture, Selected Writings,* ed. David Frisby and Mike Featherstone (London: SAGE Publications, 1997), p. 219 [first published as "Alpenreisen," *Die Zeit* (Vienna), 4, 13 July 1895].

Third day lunch and rest

WMCR: V255 / 6068

On the Simpson River

there's an article on books: on "the classics of fox-hunting literature." Tex's story "Rams" follows a regular feature of the magazine—"Estates of American Sportsmen,"—which displayed lavish homes in places like the Hamptons, the world of F. Scott Fitzgerald rather than Jack London. And in these pages we occasionally find a full-page ad for "Banff...Social Capital of the Rockies." The text assures you, "you'll meet your peers here": it is the "rendezvous for smart society...dancing with a corking 10-piece orchestra ...Canada's social center, accustomed to pleasing royalty."

Later issues feature advertisements for the Bell & Howell Filmo movie cameras, starting at $120 so you can record your feats, and there are ads for 20-, 30-, and 60-day Alaska Hunting Expeditions for the Kodiak Bear:

"THE TROPHY OF TROPHIES is a beautiful rug of the KODIAK BEAR, the largest of the carnivorous animals on earth, the king of all big game, and the subject of a thousand interesting fireside tales."

And,

"Hardships are unknown on our expeditions. Bring your wife along and let her enjoy it with you."

Tex's expeditions were grittier, and as we learn in more than one story, he is a bit suspicious of having wives along, but his trips were still about bagging the trophy and generating the heroic "fireside tale."

In a sense these are fireside stories. Part of the appeal is that the reader is placed in the position of Tex's confidant. As with the Pipestone Letters, the stories allow us to laugh at the dudes, identify with the wranglers and guides. It is a time-honoured strategy, one Tex wouldn't even have had to think of as a writer. As we join the conga line of motorhomes ambling like pack horses down the Icefields Parkway we wish we could banish all the tourists, exorcising the thought that they are us. So the readers of *The Sportsman* would have enjoyed chuckling at the British toffs who were so busy with their marmalade they missed a good shot at a bear, and they would have recognized themselves in Doc, the seasoned hunter who is no longer a Pilgrim but a friend, and almost an equal, even if he does bring a wife.

———————— • ————————

THERE IS ANOTHER ROW of houses between Tex's house and the Bow River, but there would not have been in his day, and Tex would have been able to take his morning coffee out front and watch the sun streaming through the gap between Rundle and Tunnel Mountain. But we don't see Banff in these stories, that's merely where the train stops. Tex never mentions Tunnel Mountain, in fact he mentions few places by name, and what is remarkable is how little sense of particular place there is in the stories. You might expect Tex to say something about the turrets of Castle Mountain—-red, crenellated, standing out from the grey limestone slabs of the Sawback Range that he passed on the way to his camp. Or Glacier Lake, a turquoise oval with a glaciated massif at one end, open to the treed valley at the other end, like a mini-Lake Louise. But he does not; nor does he give us a sense of distance, of how long it took to travel, say, from Banff up the 100 kilometres of trail to Saskatchewan River Crossing, and then over into Glacier Lake. And though we hear about Cliff White it is really the craziness of the newfangled sport of skiing that interests Tex. There are no portraits of locals like his first boss, Fred Brewster, or his contemporary Jimmy Simpson. But that's not Tex's intent. He is not writing local history, nor, as Howard O'Hagan would do at the end of the decade up in Jasper, writing a regional literature. Instead, Tex gives us separate episodes in an undefined mountain West.

That may have been deliberate. The editors of the magazine often blurred the context. The photos with the stories usually are not of Banff (though "Us Winter Sports" does have pictures of skiers and the Assiniboine cabin), and "Tepee Tales" features a cowboy on a palomino—a saddle horse, not a pack horse—posed on a desert bluff mesa that is obviously in the American southwest. Tex is not writing the local because he is not writing for locals. He did not publish in Canadian magazines; his audience is thousands of miles away, and the lack of specific detail gives the pieces a universal quality.

But there is more than editorial direction or commercial constraint at work here. In 1931 Canada's unemployment rate jumped to 25 per cent and something had to be done with the transient men. J.B. Harkin, Dominion Parks Commissioner, had long dreamed of a road from Banff to Jasper, to bring in the new tourists who were turning from the railway to the automobile. During the First World War "enemy aliens" had been used to work on the road from Banff to Lake Louise. Now camps for the unemployed were set up to extend that road. Hundreds of men were assembled in the fall of 1931 at either end of the road, survey teams were sent through to mark the route, and the clearing of brush and stumps began. In 1932 as Tex was beginning his Pipestone Letters, road crews with picks and shovels were hacking through the forest toward Bow Lake. By 1934 they had completed 57 miles (95 kilometres) of road, with another 90 miles to go. In 1938 a young man who had hiked the trail the year before wrote enthusiastically in *Maclean's* magazine that,

By the end of the 1937 season, there was open to tourists some seventy-five miles of completed road on the Jasper end [to Sunwapta Pass], and about forty-five miles on the Banff end [to Waterfowl Lakes]...It is expected that very soon this great tourist thoroughfare, ten years in the building, will be completed.[2]

In 1939 the first truck lumbered through and the highway opened officially in June 1940, celebrated in an eleven-minute NFB film. This "great tourist thoroughfare" was a gravel track 18 feet [not quite six metres] wide, but compared to the horse trails Tex had used it would have felt like a six-lane freeway. Even as he was writing, his milieu was already the past. His later stories were published in the *National Sportsman*, which sold for 10¢, and *Hunting and Fishing*, which was only 5¢: much more a middle-class magazine, it had ads for tobacco, guns, fishing gear, outboard motors instead of yachts, and instead of champagne, beer in cans.

By the time Tex wrote his last story, he was preparing to move out of the house on Spray Avenue and out of the valley he had worked in and loved. The wider world was changing throughout 1938 as well: Neville Chamberlain was meeting Hitler at Berchtesgaden; in Hungary Lazlo Biro had invented the ballpoint pen and was preparing to flee the Nazis to Argentina (Tex wrote his stories out in pencil or fountain pen, in a neat longhand); in Winnipeg they were founding the Winnipeg Ballet, and in Orillia, Gordon Lightfoot was being born.

It is always the end of an era, but some demarcations are sharper than others. We are lucky to have these snapshots of life on the trail before the trail became a highway. Indeterminate of place and time, just slightly tinged with nostalgia, they occupy the nebulous zone between reportage and myth.

Ted Bishop
28 September 2007
Edmonton / Banff / Budapest

2. Edward E. Bishop, "Mountain Road," *Maclean's*, July 15, 1938, 24.

Dad (Nello Vernon-Wood) with animal skins

INTRODUCTION

———————————— • ————————————

The journey of Nello Vernon-Wood (1882–1978) was the opposite of that stock figure in North America: the rogue from a modest background who invents exalted social origins after arriving in the New World, where no-one can call his bluff. Nello was a gentleman born and bred, according to contemporary definitions. And yet his story and the stories he wrote about the New World and his place in it are much more than another version of Tarzan-of-the-Apes. His reinvention of himself as 'Tex Wood' (or Woods), an authentic western Canadian man both in his daily life (at least to some extent) and in his homespun tales of a vanishing era, has much to tell us today about how the West was not just won, but also created as a fantasy for many people who wanted (and want) to believe that the modern (industrialized) world itself can be left behind. In this, he was like two other popular writers of his time, Grey Owl and Chief Buffalo Child Long Lance. The Englishman Archie Belaney became a best-selling Canadian author when he took the name Grey Owl and lived as an aboriginal. Sylvester Clark Long had been treated as an African-American in his birthplace, the American South, because he was of mixed race. As the Blackfoot Chief Buffalo Child Long Lance, he became a popular author of "Indian" stories for American and Canadian newspapers and magazines.[1] Also like his contemporaries Grey Owl and Long Lance, in his writing, and in the persona he invented for it, Tex Wood created an image of the frontier that was a rough-and-ready and above-all, an authentically wild

1. See Jane Billinghurst, *Grey Owl: The Many Faces of Archie Belaney* (Vancouver: Greystone Books, 1999) and Donald B. Smith, *Chief Buffalo Child Long Lance: The Glorious Imposter* (Red Deer, AB: Red Deer Press, 1999).

place because he could pass as a member of that world. This world, often called "the Old West," was a place of infinite possibilities.

As Patricia Limerick points out, "[in] the search to distinguish 'the Real West' from 'the Fake West'...the Real West and the Fake West end up tied together, virtually Siamese twins sharing the same circulatory system."Along with many other writers of his time, Tex helped to knit together the West of his guiding experiences with the West as a literary object. It is not possible to tell, therefore, the difference between the "authentic" West (and its authentic author, Tex) and the "fake" West. In Tex's writings, both are real.[2] As we will show, Tex even "winked" at his readers in some of his stories to show that he was not as authentically backwoods as some might think. But he, and the West he helped popularize, seemed real enough—or entertaining enough—to ensure a steady appetite for his stories in sporting journals like *The Sportsman* and *The Forum*, slick magazines produced for a middle-class readership on the eastern seaboard of the United States.

During the early part of the twentieth century, when Tex was writing stories and working as a guide, people flocked to the Canadian and American frontiers to have an experience of a world they thought was lost: a place of adventure where civilization did not seem to have taken hold. And if they could not go there, they read stories about that romantic place by people who really lived there and who could tell them what it was really like. Tex was and presented himself as the tough old frontiersman that his readers wanted or needed to imagine. In other words, Tex could "pass" as a man of the wilds. Elaine K. Ginsberg points out "the positive potential of passing [is] a way of challenging ... categories and boundaries. In its politics, passing has the potential to create a space for creative self-determination and agency: the opportunity to create multiple identities, to experiment with multiple subject positions, and to cross social and economic boundaries that exclude or oppress."[3] Tex Wood deliberately created a persona and a life that freed him from the decidedly unadventurous constraints of his upper-class family life in England—and which he was later able to use as a writer because it fit and/or fed the fantasies of his readers. But, as we shall

2. Patricia Limerick, "The Real West." In *The Real West*, commentary by Patricia Nelson Limerick, introduction by Andrew E. Masich (Denver: Civic Center Cultural Complex, 1996) 13–22.

3. Elaine K. Ginsberg, *Passing and the Fictions of Identity* (Durham, NC: Duke University Press, 1996) 16.

see, a close examination Tex's use of language in many of his stories shows traces of his education and upbringing from that previous life, mixed in with "Old West" turns of phrase, just as habits from his life in England remained part of his daily life as a man of the mountains.

Tex was born to a family that was at the very least genteel, in Stratford-upon-Avon in 1882. One family snapshot[4] shows him outside the gates of a country house, with his mother Ruth Hunter and aunt; he told family members that it was his family home, but he almost never spoke of his family. His father, an army physician, is said to have been killed in Egypt within a decade of his birth. Nello was named after his maiden aunt Nell, who helped to raise him. In his early twenties, Nello "lit out for the territories," landing in Ontario in 1903, where he worked as a hand on an isolated farm somewhere between Kingston and Trenton.[5] He left that hard life for the Canadian West, going first to Medicine Hat, where he arrived by 1904.

Nello was charged with manslaughter at Medicine Hat in late 1904 or 1905. He had pursued and fired on a Métis man ('halfbreed', as he would have been called then) who had stolen a horse belonging to Tex. After a lengthy struggle for his life, the man survived and the charge was dropped.[6] The judge, it seems, had known Vernon-Wood senior, who seems to have served in Canada at some point, perhaps with Wolseley's Red River Expedition in 1870, or in 1882, or perhaps even on Middleton's Expedition (1885) against the Riel uprising.[7] Not surprisingly, given the bonds of class, ethnicity, and privilege, Nello was paroled under the watchful eye of his mother, whom the judge summoned from England to stand surety for her unruly son. She arrived and had a large, comfortable house built for them. A year or so later, the terms of the parole satisfied, she returned to England. When she became ill, Nello went home to England to see his mother (who was to die of stomach cancer in 1906 or 1907). He

4. In the possession of Nello's grand-daughter Sonja Vernon-Wood, daughter of Christina Vernon-Wood, Lee Creek, BC.

5. See "Tex Vernon-Wood. Recollections by his Grandson, John R. Gow" in Appendix A.

6. According to Christina Vernon-Wood, in a private communication with Andrew Gow in 2003. Her source was her husband Bill, Nello's son.

7. The Wolseley connection is plausible because Vernon-Wood senior is said to have died in Egypt soon after Nello's birth: Major-General Sir Garnet Wolseley also led an expedition to Egypt in 1882 to put down the Urabi Revolt, and then commanded the Nile Expedition to relieve General Gordon at Khartoum in 1884.

left the Medicine Hat house in the care of a friend, returning a few months later to find the house deserted and emptied of its lavish furnishings. He sold the house and moved on to the Rocky Mountains, first to handle the horses used in the construction of the tramway up to Lake Louise.

In 1906 or 1907, Tex went to Banff, ostensibly to take the waters at the Springs to help heal a broken leg that had resulted from an accident when "a horse fell on him."[8] It was there that he met Jim Brewster, who offered him a job in the outfitting business.[9] Sometime in this period he earned the name Tex for a set of snazzy Texas riding chaps he affected, perhaps for practicality, perhaps to hide his egregious Englishness—a quality then not much in demand in the Canadian West.[10] He later said that he preferred to be called Tex, finding Nello "Shakespearean" and too high-flown for his taste.[11] He claims that he had all kinds of fights and grief as a child on account of the name: "My mother had been reading Dante or some bloody thing," he said in a good-natured way in an interview in 1969.[12] It would seem that "Shakespearean" in this context meant both "English" and "elite." Sarah Carter has pointed out that abiding colonial insecurities about Englishness were related to both ethnicity and class, citing J.S. Woodsworth's judgement that "the Scotch, Irish and Welsh have

8. From taped interviews made by Maryalice H. Stewart, 17 January and 2 February, 1969, at the wmcr: Reel S1/17 A, 1, accession number 1713.

9. *Banff Crag and Canyon*, Obituary for N. Vernon-Wood, May 17, 1978; also taped interview, wmcr S1/17 A, 2.

10. See, for example, Mark Zuehlke, *Scoundrels, Dreamers & Second Sons: British Remittance Men in the Canadian West* (Vancouver/Toronto: Whitecap Books, 1994), e.g., p. 60: "The popular Canadian folklore that grew up around the presence of British remittance men in the Canadian west represented them as fools, drunkards, louts, scoundrels, and snobs who refused to fit into the evolving Canadian society. The British gentleman was derided in bars, satirized on stage, lampooned in books, savaged in the music halls, and generally treated with scorn." For a very thorough treatment of this topic in the Canadian West, see Patrick A. Dunae, *Gentleman Immigrants: From the British Public Schools to the Canadian Frontier* (Vancouver/Toronto: Douglas & McIntyre, 1981), esp. chapters VI, Nature's Gentlemen and VII, Remittance Men. In the interview with Maryalice Stewart, Tex explains that he had made a good deal of money working on a pack train at an Idaho gold mine and spent some of his earnings on a fancy set of batwing (Texas-style) chaps on his way back to Lake Louise. As he was reticent about his unusual first name, he did not use it, and Jim Macleod decided to call him Tex because of the chaps. wmcr S1/17 A, 17.

11. Cf. note 3, John Gow's recollections; confirmed by Christina Vernon-Wood, in a private communication with Andrew Gow in 2003.

12. Stewart makes it clear that she had never heard the name Nello before, only the "N." in "N. Vernon-Wood." wmcr S1/17 A, 12.

A hunting party, 1924

WMCR: V255 / 6068

Banff in winter, 1928

WMCR: V255 / 6068

done well. The greater number of failures has been among the English... On many western farms, certain Englishmen have proved so useless that when help is needed, 'no Englishmen need apply'." Both the "failures of English cities" (working-class immigrants) and upper-class "remittance men" were equally unwelcome and scorned.[13]

Nello's childhood experience with animals (he had kept ferrets for hunting, and later a large hunting dachshund called Snapper) and especially with horses, seems to have stood him in good stead in Banff, where he worked as a horse wrangler, hunting guide, outfitter, and later park warden. While he was working for the Brewsters as a guide, a client shot an animal outside the law, and Tex "took a fall for the Brewster outfit in 1912" (with a conviction for poaching) but was "reputable enough by 1919 [sic] to pin on a badge" as a Park Warden.[14] He was soon assigned to Massive, a halt on the C.P.R. east of Banff, whence he visited town weekly in winter with a dogsled. His baby daughter Dorothy's first words, she claimed, were "Mush! mush!"

According to Cyndi Smith, Tex was with the Park Service at an earlier date than 1919—the date Sid Marty gives: "The Dominion Park Service assigned one of their wardens, Tex Vernon-Wood, usually called Tex Wood, to assist the Walcotts in 1917."[15] The earlier date makes sense because in 1969, he said he set up an outfit of his own in 1919.[16] He had worked for Charles Walcott since at least 1911, as Byron Harmon's photograph of the guides on the Smithsonian Expedition of that year attests.[17] The Smithsonian Expedition was one of the most famous scientific expeditions into the mountains at the time, and it provided material for Tex's later stories. Its members included Mary M. Vaux, a Quaker mountaineer, geologist and botanist from Philadelphia, and her husband Charles D. Walcott, a

13. Sarah Carter, "Britishness, 'Foreignness', Women and Land in Western Canada 1890s–1920s" in *Humanities Research* XIII, 1 (2006), 43–60; here 48–49; cited from J.S. Woodsworth, *Strangers Within Our Gates* (Toronto: F.C. Stephenson, 1909), 51 and 52.

14. Sid Marty, *A Grand and Fabulous Notion: The First Century of Canada's Parks* (Toronto: NC Press, 1984).

15. Cyndi Smith, *Off the Beaten Track: Women Adventurers and Mountaineers in Western Canada* (Jasper, AB: Coyote Books, 1989). See also Colleen Skidmore, ed., *This Wild Spirit: Women in the Rocky Mountains of Canada* (Edmonton, AB: University of Alberta Press, 2006), especially on Mary Vaux.

16. Taped interview, S1/17 B, 31.

17. See Frontispiece.

geologist and palaeontologist who worked for the Smithsonian Institution. Vaux had met Walcott when he was working on his renowned discovery, the Burgess Shale. Tex would later turn an annoying encounter with a game warden while hunting (legally) in the Park for the Smithsonian's collection with Vaux and Walcott into a story, "Tex Reads his Permit."

Another echo of his work with this illustrious pair surfaces in "This Guiding Game," in which one of Tex's wranglers surprised a professor of geology with an intimate knowledge of the geology of the Rocky Mountains. Tex maintained an association with the Walcotts for many years. "After he quit the government and acquired his own pack outfit in 1919, Tex continued to escort them on their summer expeditions from Lake Louise... Mary was a very determined woman and the first time Tex outfitted for them he told her in no uncertain terms that 'I was quite open to suggestions but I was running the pack outfit, after which she left him alone'."[18] Clearly, Tex was independent and utterly undaunted by the elite clientele that came his way, principally from the upper echelons of U.S., and sometimes British, "society." In the Whyte Museum of the Canadian Rockies, among his personal papers, is a carbon copy of a letter one of his New York customers had written to another American, recommending Tex as a guide because he was "a gentleman" and thus fit company for women as well as men.[19] "I'd go to New York and go to their clubs, and they'd introduce me around. I had a whole clientele of New York lawyers," he said in 1969.[20] Tex made his living this way for some years, and guiding Roosevelts, Fleishmans, and other well-heeled clients kept him and his family comfortably in a frame house on Spray Avenue in Banff through the 1920s and 1930s. He took the yeast magnate Max Fleischman, whom he had met in California, hunting for trophy sheep. Though they did not shoot anything (no adequate trophy horns having presented themselves to their gunsights) they had a wonderful time stalking sheep.[21]

Eventually the Park boundaries expanded, and former hunting grounds, including Tex's beloved Pipestone River Valley, were off limits to his hunting guests. In 1938, his business "was getting impossible" and he moved to the Columbia Valley, setting up the Edgewood Ranch (apparently named

18. This is a verbatim citation from an interview taped 2 February, 1969: S1/17 C, 22.

19. M 77/1.

20. Taped interview, S1/17 C, 16.

21. Taped interview, S1/17 C, 27.

On the trail, 1924

for his parents' house in Stratford) on the benchlands above Invermere, BC, as a combined ranching operation and summer camp for the children of his guiding clients ("boys with too much money and a little spoiled"). He got in touch with a school in Richfield, Connecticut, and in spring he went there "to meet the parents so they could see what kind of an egg I was."[22] The name "Dirk Roosevelt," one of the well-heeled campers, could still be seen decades later on one of the frame guest cabins on the ranch. Tex eventually moved from this property at the end of the Second World War, taking the Edgewood name with him to a ranch on fertile valley bottomland near Brisco, BC. He eventually sold this outfit too and moved in semi-retirement to Windermere, BC, where he worked for some years as a fire lookout on Mount Swansea, 6,200 feet above the Columbia Valley, and later as a Parks employee well into his late 70s.

Despite Tex's rugged life and self-fashioned image as a tough outdoorsman, he never completely abandoned his first identity as an educated English gentleman. He was a life-long subscriber to the overseas edition of the *Manchester Guardian* and a social democrat in a world of rugged individualists. He read widely[23] and this probably suggested numerous models and possibilities for his own writing style. He began publishing stories around 1930, after the expansion of Banff National Park had consumed his old guiding and hunting territories around Shadow Lake and the Pipestone Canyon. The stories, mainly written in the persona of a rough-and-tumble guide, complete with varying approximations of "western" dialect, kept coming throughout the Depression (1930–1938). They were clearly a means to help feed his fairly large family. After publishing in *The Sportsman*, he was solicited to write for other magazines, including *The Forum*,[24] the editor of which asked for stories to be written in

22. S1/17 C, 29.

23. See "A Gift from Grandad Vernon-Wood," by his grandson Harry W. Gow in Appendix B. In the piece entitled "Dried Spinach or Moose Steak?,". composed as a letter to a friend in New York from "N. Vernon-Wood" and published in *Hunting and Fishing*, June 1935, we get a sense of Tex's appetite for reading: "Thanks for the magazines an newspapers. Last winter, we was stormbound so much that I learnt all of the Stockman's Almanac by heart, an most of the Government's report on grasshopper control. I sure was pinin for a change of thought. —*Yours truly*, Tex." In 1969, he noted that his unusual name, Nello, seemed to be Italian as it appeared in the work of Dante and. perhaps of Bocaccio, of which he had a translation. Taped interview, WMCR, S1/17 A, 12.

24. Letter of October 20, 1930, from the editor, Harry Goddard Leach, to Tex: "How would you like to try an 1800-word Travelogue for *The Forum* on 'Big Game Hunting in the

"picturesque language," and the *National Sportsman*.[25] Tex's writing styles betray both his social origins and his aspirations—partly to some acceptable form of Western Anglo-Canadian (but not English!) normativity, which required a measure of downward mobility in the social sense. However, the erudite jokes and allusions in Tex's stories make it clear that this is no hick writing: it is a "gent"sort of pretending to be a hick.

Tex also wrote a number of "straight" pieces in his first persona, that of an educated English gentleman. One was a hunting story, "Rams," published in *The Sportsman*, April 1931, 67–68; here he betrays a classical education with an allusion to the first line of Caesar's *De bello gallica:*

All visitors are divided into three parts like ancient Gaul: "tourists," "tin canners," and "pilgrims." Any old visitor is a tourist provided he or she comes by train. The tin canners explain themselves, but as soon as one mounts a cayuse and takes to the hills with an outfit, to hunt, fish, climb, or just loaf, then he or she becomes a pilgrim, and as such is accepted into the inner circle.

Another straight piece, "An Early Ski Attempt on Mt. Ptarmigan," published soon after in the *Canadian Alpine Journal,* the official organ of the Canadian Alpine Club[26] and written under the name N. Vernon-Wood, is clearly a product of an English education, with (what was at the time) a gentle and natural use of scriptural language: "A day spent in intimate contact with almost overwhelming grandeur is reward pressed down and running over." (p. 97; cf. Luke 6:38). His style is otherwise just as elegant but nonetheless suited to the grandeur of the subject as he notes the names and social class of members of another skiing party: "In March of last year [1931], A.N.T. Rankin, of London, England, and his wife, Lady Jean, accompanied by two of the original climbers made a ski ascent of Ptarmigan." (p. 99). If we compare this with the language he used in "Us Winter Sports" in *The Sportsman*, for instance, we find a very different voice, even though the topic, skiing, is the same:

Things didn't go too awful bad until we hit the first hill. It's steep and the trail

---

Rockies.' You can work in some of your most exciting experiences. And if you will use your own most pictu[r]esque language, and do not stumble into academic English, thinking it is for *The Forum*, you might produce something very original and refreshing for our readers. We will be willing to gamble $35.00 on the experiment, anyhow." wmcr, M 77/1.

25. Letter of May 5, 1932, from E.W. Smith, Managing Editor, to Tex, asking for an 1800-word piece and "some good clear photographs, both action and scenic." wmcr, M 77/1

26. *Canadian Alpine Journal,* vol. 21, 1932, 135–138.

makes a bend at the bottom. The Bull [Mountie] takes off first, and makes it pretty good. Buckshot follows, but his pack gets going faster than he is, so he sits down, by way of putting on the brakes. I shove off, and pass Buck like a bat out of hell, but can't make that turn. I try stem turns, jump turns, telemarks, and a lot that ain't in our book, and finish in a nose dive, with kind of a tail spin, and come to a perfect fourteen-point landing, losing hide on all fourteen of 'em, believe it or not.[27]

The last story he had published appeared in the *National Sportsman* in October, 1938. His daughter-in-law Christina asked him later in life about the end ("around 1939") of his writing career: "Dad, could you do it [write] again?" The answer was "No—I don't think I would be capable of it. It was there—and then it left."[28]

This piece and many others of the dozens published in such magazines skate awfully close to what we could call "class minstrelsy," and away from "passing," since Tex was not at all the homespun, rather rough working-class character who speaks in so many of his stories for popular magazines. It was as if he were—metaphorically—in "black-face," the makeup that white actors like Al Jolson wore in early twentieth-century vaudeville productions when they were expected to play African-American characters. Just as it was clear to vaudeville audiences at the time that black-face was not real, so it might have been just as clear to Tex's readers that he could not be one of his own semi-literate characters; it was enough that the language sounded authentic according to the standards of the day. This language, although it might have led some clients to think that Tex had always been a frontiersman, "winks" at an audience which was expected to enjoy the conceit while understanding that it was constructed, rather than natural.

Sometimes that need to sound authentic, even to the point of caricature, creates views of aboriginal people and new immigrants in Tex's writing that are caricatures in themselves. Today, it is impossible to see Tex's portrayals of Indians, Chinese laundrymen, and foreigners as much more than stereotypes. But in the literature of Canada that was published before the Second World War, stereotypes were an essential part of its fiction and non-fiction for mass audiences. Although Tex's ironic tone suggests that he might have wanted us to be repelled by the coarseness of his characters' views, they were more common than we might like to admit. If we compare his tone to Emily Carr's in *Klee Wyck* of 1941, we see that she too was able

27. Jan. 1931, pp. 44–45; 45.

28. According to Christina Vernon-Wood, in a private communication with AG in 2003.

Bow Park

to caricature aboriginal people and yet on the same page convey a strong sense of how "noble" she thought they were.[29] In *Janey Canuck in the West* of 1910, Emily Murphy—in her persona as Janey Canuck, intrepid Anglo-Canadian traveller—makes fun of recent immigrants and at many points expresses her dismay about their filthiness.[30] Thomas Chandler Haliburton's satirical lampooning of Americans in *The Clockmaker* series of 1836 and Susannah Moodie's stereotyping of Americans, Scotsmen, and and Irishmen in *Roughing It in the Bush* (1852) use similar stereotypical devices that are just not funny today.

Fictional work about the Canadian West also included stereotypical portraits of uncouth immigrants and Indians, partly (as in the best-selling novels of Ralph Connor from the early twentieth century) to show how genteel the "real" Canadians could be. Tex's work betrays many of the same influences and sentiments, although his more positive portrayals of aboriginal people are more reminiscent of Grey Owl's approach. There are various references to Indians in Tex's stories, and none of them is hostile or judgemental; some are clearly positive, though most have some air of stereotype about them. In his serious piece, "Rams," he notes that the Indians in the Banff area are very good hunters and have a pragmatic view of guns, rather than making a fetish of the supposed differences, as wealthy hunters do: "Any gun good, shootem good," that is, any gun is a good one if you shoot it well.

In "Sawback and the Sporting Proposition," the Tex character tells his friend Sawback about a fish round-up by aboriginal people that he witnessed at Long Lake in the Cariboo: the women make holes and set nets at one end of the lake, which he says is four miles long and 500 yards wide; then the men gallop their horses on to the ice at the other end, all the way along the lake, driving the fish into the nets, which he admires for its efficiency but also calls "unsportin'," of course. In "It's Good to be Alive," he approves of aboriginal thrift regarding the meat of wild animals and identifies with their practices: "when it comes to salvagin' meat, I'm a reg'lar Indian. Nothin' burns me up like the eggs who drop a prime animal, an' then just saw offen the head, an' leave the meat for the Coyotes an' Wolverines." In "This Guiding Game," Tex appeals to aboriginal practices, but his client,

29. Emily Carr, *Klee Wyck* (Toronto: Penguin, 2006) originally published in 1941 by the University of Toronto Press.

30. Emily Murphy, *Janey Canuck in the West* (London: Cassell, 1910).

an uppity professor of geology, is not convinced: "Then I tried to tell him the difference between a tepee and a tent, and explained that the Indians had been using them for some considerable time, and that they cooked in 'em and everything, but it was no go." His character uses the derogatory term "Nitchies" (now archaic) for Indians[31] once, probably because that was the sort of word a mountain man might have been expected to use; the context reveals no particular disrespect (on the contrary, Tex is making sarcastic remarks about the professor of geology).

When Tex's Anglo-Canadian characters distance themselves from Indians or "foreign" people, pushing them to the margins, we might read this an expression of Tex's own desire to "pass" as a man of the people and a man of the mountains,[32] to efface his class origins and his Englishness. As Daniel Coleman has argued in *White Civility*, other Canadian writers for popular audiences—most notably Ralph Connor—had featured English characters who learned to be manly on the Canadian frontier, but who were also obliged to make "foreigners" understand how to be a real man in Canada, which includes being a gentleman when the circumstances warrant. This form of frontier manliness is a form of "muscular Christianity," and it involves having physical strength as well as strength of character. Upper-class Englishmen were not thought to have much of either.

As early as 1909, J.S. Woodsworth had argued in *Strangers Within Our Gates*, that the best English immigrants were working-class, and that even these people were inferior to sturdy peasant stock.[33] Tex clearly understood that being an upper-class Englishman was not a good thing in Western Canada. In order to pass, and become a "real" Canadian of humbler origins, he had to put "foreigners" in their place in his writing and attenuate his own foreignness. Tex clearly did this in his own life by avoiding his real name, by means of the nickname he started using early in the century, by his marriage to a working-class Irishwoman and by his Western-style clothing. Many of his stories also seem to be part of an active desire to articulate Western authenticity and nativeness (if not quite "nativity");

31. See William C. Richardson, "Nitchies" in *Notes and Queries* series 9, vol. xii (1903), 227 and 278.

32. In "Fifth Avenue Pilgrims Amid the Goats," Tex describes himself in an exchange with a customer as a "mountain man."

33. See Daniel Coleman's discussion of civility and masculinity in *White Civility: The Literary Project of English Canada* (Toronto: University of Toronto Press, 2006) 22–23 and 128–140.

RNWMP with Dad

WMCR: V255 / PD 15

but then in most of them, his use of high-flown vocabulary, mock-lofty, and cleverly twisted clichés suggests a man of letters behind it all. Mainly he was concerned, as his grandson John Gow put it (see Appendix A), to distance himself from his English origins. The clearest efforts in this direction are "William, Prepare my Barth" and "What's in a Name?" in which he pokes fun at upper-class Englishmen:

When it comes to hitting the trails de lux, though, it takes an Englishman to do it up brown, with butter on both sides. I got me a brace of Woodbiners before the war, and they brought everything except the brick house. They had a chest of silver, and a valet to see that we didn't pinch the spoons, and fill the bathtub. Their tents would hold a round-up crew and were as heavy as a green cook's bannock. The tents had telescope poles, with wooden hickeys to screw on top of the uprights, painted red, white, and blue. That was to show us bally Colonials where we got off at. Their rifles assayed $500 to the ton, and there was anyway $2,000 worth of them.

The crowning touch is this paragraph, a malicious send-up of the British "Great White Hunter":

They used to tell us yarns about hunting in India and Africa, where they had a million misguided heathens herd the game past a couple of Morris chairs, in the shade of the fig trees, and then they would take their rifle from the second assistant rifle wallah and plug the galloping gazelle as he fogged by.

Tex also calls himself a Canuck in "Us Winter Sports": "but that's the trouble with us Canucks—never know when we are beat, till somebody pounds it in with a neck yoke," suggesting that Canadians are both stubborn and stupid, but noble and tough all the same. On the other hand, Sawback addresses Tex in "What's in a Name?" as an Englishman:

"Far be it from me," says Sawback Smith, "to cast any aspersions on your nationality, feller, but you gotta admit that huntin' with some of these here County families is what curdles the milk of human kindness, an' frays to hell the cinch that binds the Empire."

Thus Tex refers to himself as a "Colonial" and a "Canuck"—but he is also addressed (and thus perceived) as an Englishman. Vernon-Wood never lost his gentle, precise Midlands British pronunciation (nor a sibilant whistle between his teeth when he pronounced the letter s), as one can hear in the hours of taped interviews and stories also preserved in the Whyte Museum.

Tex also used another *nom de plume*, "Ramon Chesson," clearly a calque of his own Anglo-Italian moniker, with a Spanish first name and WASP last name ("The Wild Goose Chase," set in the "south [New] Jersey lowlands"!). This story is also clearly the work of an educated writer:

I hauled out my watch and leaned over to get the glow of Hank's cigarette on the dial. "Still plenty of time to wait," I announced. Hank got up, shook off the snow, and looked out at the white marsh. Then he settled back in the flimsy blind and puffed away. For stoicism, Epictetus was a bush leaguer.

Again, we glimpse the educated gentleman who refers to classical philosophers casually, even colloquially, in the great outdoors. To support his creation of an authentic frontier voice, in most of the magazine stories Tex used non-standard spelling to indicate rough frontier diction or dialect. One senses that he is presenting us with an alter ego, an "inner Tex," who at least *thinks* in this style, even if Nello himself never expressed himself in it. His exaggerated diction shows that this persona is a construct. He was also writing for a market that relished the (to us) hokey diction and style of cowboy romance. However, there is much more to his style than hoke: in "Sawback and the Sporting Proposition," he treats us to this virtuoso piece of macaronic false hickery:

"Do tell! Well, there's also a fardel of fish down where Skookumchuck Crick empties into the lake. I dunno about you, but I'm fed up on lean venison, so I rid over to see if you'd consider postponin' your various inutile pursuits, an' concentrate on decoyin' the odd Cristivomer outer his native element. Today's the 14th of May, you benighted old bullhead, an' lake fishin' opens tomorrow."

"Lightenin' Lucifer!" I exclaim. "I'd plumb lost track of the days..."

Next mornin' we leave Sawback's dugout before dawn had even commenced to crack, and make the ten or so parasangs to the mouth of Skookumchuck in less'n three hours, which is right good goin' when you consider we got a pack pony loaded with various housekeepin' utensils, a tepee, an' a pair of 90 x 90 flea bags.

"Inutile," "Christivomer," and "parasangs" were not in the vocabulary of ordinary fishing guides then, and they are not now either. The joke is clear only to the educated reader who can put together the quaint expressions ("Lightenin' Lucifer!") and grammar ("I rid over") with the recondite vocabulary and such elegant "false hick-isms" as "onmerited" or "before the dawn had even commenced to crack" in order to "get" all the various levels of linguistic jokes, cliché-wrangling, and language games the author is playing. An inflatable boat is by turns "newmatick," a "wherry," a "caique," a "coracle," a "pneumatic punt," an "aerated ark," a "danged dugout," and a "shallop"; "cussing" is "maledication an' imprecation"; the "Siawash"[34] are "red brethren" and "noble aborigine[s]"; and their horses' feet pound on the lake "like the drums of Tophet."[35]

In "Fifth Avenue Pilgrims Amid the Goats," also with Tex as narrator, to vary the language when talking about mountain goats, he refers to them as *Ovis Canadensis*. In "It's Good to be Alive," Tex reports "Me an' the Pilgrim got going right celerious after breakfast," which he later refers to as "matutinal flapjacks," as he longs for supper, or "vespers." In "Sawback Cleans a Laker," his clients are "Piscatorial Pilgrims." In "Navigatin' for Namaycush," Tex uses an Italian phrase and in the same breath makes fun of it, of himself and of the reader by suggesting that it's Spanish: "It seems like a right pious idea. I shore need a change, an' settin' in a boat draggin' a spoon on the end of a line sounds right *dolce far niente*, as they say in Ensenada, so I lets myself in for it." In "Tex Takes a Trophy," more of his Biblical learning comes through when the Tex-persona, writing to a friend in New York, lets him know "I don't give three whoops in Sheol if" Yet there was not a pretentious bone in his body. In "The Guide Knows Everything," he makes fun of himself, of educated people in general, and of guides as well:

An' every once in a while some bird will pull something like this: "Look at that view, Tex; don't you think Corot would have loved to paint it, or do you think Browning would have caught the atmosphere better—or do you?" When they start that sort of thing, it's a good plan to grab your field glasses plumb excited an' say, "Holy old doodle, they's a bear on that slide—no, b'gosh, it's a burned stump. Don't it beat hell how them shadders fool you sometimes?

There is more than a hint of P.G. Wodehouse or Walt Kelly's immortal cartoon *Pogo* in his ironic use of mixed high-flown and everyday or backwoodsy diction. Today, Tex's sly comic style looks like an attempt to call attention to the very thing that he sometimes tried to hide: the fact that he does not belong, and that this non-belonging gives him sharp insight about the world around him, and the privileged world he came from.

34. 'Siwash' is a term for aboriginal people in Chinook jargon, derived from French *sauvage*. This widespread racist insult was still used by ranchers in the BC interior within living memory to refer to all aboriginal people. See "Bill Casselman's Canadian Word of the Day": http://www.billcasselman.com/cwod_archive/siwash_updated.htm, accessed 4 June, 2007.

35. 2 Kings 23, 10 and Jeremiah 19.

Tex himself did not live conventionally in an urban setting with an occasional foray into the mountains for sport, as the casual reader of his piece in the *Canadian Alpine Journal* might have assumed. He was a working man who started out as a horse-wrangler, and was afterwards an outfitter, a guide, a park ranger, and a rancher. He married across class and religious lines: Joan Raill (or Real, or Reilly, or even O'Reilly, depending on the document), an Irish Catholic chambermaid from the district of Annascaul, County Kerry, the daughter of a fisherman, who was working at the Banff Springs Hotel when they met, and then married in 1912. He told her after they were married that he had "only two requirements: tea at 11:00 and lunch at 1:00."[36] He might have learned to read (and cite) Scripture as part of a conventional Church of England childhood, and he might have taken "elevenses" every day, but he chose a very different world to live and work in. In a certain sense, Tex straddled the privileged world of his childhood and the world of hard work and social and religious inferiority (as his associations would have been seen at the time). He goes out of his way in one story to distinguish himself and his friends (waddies, proletariat, commoners) from the aristocratic owner of one lodge who refused to allow hunting in the area he had leased ("Dried Spinach or Moose Steak?"); and in "The Last Great Buffalo Drive" he refers to himself and his friends, acting as extras in a Western, as "us poor benighted hill-billies."

For Tex in most of his stories, a proper mountain man gets dirty and does not worry overly about comfort. He does not need to engage in this behaviour anywhere else; it might be alright to be a dandy in New York or London, but to be a successfully masculine man and hunter in the mountains, one must, according to Tex, forget about hygiene and appearance. These issues are central to "William, Prepare my Barth," "What's in a Name?," and "Pipestone Letter No. 1." The English gents in the first two fail to attain proper mountain masculinity, because they continue to insist on bathing, shaving, and careful dressing in the morning, thus cutting deeply into hunting time; by contrast, the well-dressed club man who arrives at the station in the latter story successfully makes the transition, with Tex's none-too-gentle help, to proper mountain masculinity, becoming both dirty and a successful hunter.

Tex's own body, repeatedly characterized as very slight ("Nobody's ever

36. According to Christina Vernon-Wood, in a private communication with AG in 2003.

complimented me on my figger; in fack, I got to stand twice in the same place before I throw a shader..."[37])—not ideally masculine, therefore—plays a role in this drama. Due to his slender build, his ability as a mountain man, and thus his "mountain masculinity," is questioned by clients on at least two occasions, in "Fifth Avenue Pilgrims Amid the Goats" and in "Pipestone Letters No. 1." Just as the "muscular Christian" teaches foreigners in Canada how to behave themselves by beating them at fisticuffs and then lecturing them about proper behaviour, so Tex's "mountain masculinity" will show that he is the real man who has a thing or two to teach the over-civilized clients about manliness. He is vindicated on both counts; in the former because the questioner himself turns out to be effeminate and dainty, and thus capable neither of getting dirty nor of being a good hunter; and in the second, because Tex successfully helps his client to attain mountain masculinity himself. In both cases, it is made clear that Tex's physical prowess is up to anything these two men can dish out, and then some. Here Tex is writing back to his clients, who doubt his skills, and therefore his masculinity. It's one of the rare times in mountain literature when the guide gets to have his say.[38]

One crack appears in this system when the Honourable Fitzwilliam Smythe-Smythe manages to kill a trophy moose without getting a bit dirty or breaking a sweat, in "What's in a Name?" one of Tex's last pieces (February 1938). Furthermore, another code of sportsmanship makes a cameo appearance in this story. The Hon. Fitz shouts before shooting his moose, to startle it—because it is unsporting to shoot a 'sitting' animal unawares (and unwise to drop it in the water where it was standing in any case).

The imperial gaze of this gentleman-gone-native must therefore be imagined as a fractured one: on the one hand, he condescends to his characters (including his own authorial persona, Tex), deliberately having

---

37. In "Navigatin for Namaycush."

38. See Tina Loo's analysis of the relationship between guides and big-game hunters in "Of Moose and Men: Hunting for Masculinities in British Columbia, 1880–1939." *The Western Historical Quarterly*, Vol. 32, No. 3. (Autumn, 2001), pp. 296–319. Loo points out that hunters often mocked guides in their articles for *Rod and Gun* and *Field and Stream*, but that guides never had a chance to talk back. See also Alec Lucas' article about nature writing and animal stories in Carl F. Klinck et al., eds., *Literary History of Canada: Canadian Literature in English* (Toronto: University of Toronto Press, 1965) pp. 364–388 for a detailed look at the genre of sporting books; Lucas notes that the emphasis in these sporting books is on "the pleasures of good fellowship and life in the open air" (372), from the perspective of sportsmen, not of guides.

them make all the mistakes his (more) educated audience would recognize and which would then have seemed to be characteristic of such "types": dangling prepositions, faulty grammar, g's dropped from the ends of words, slang, "cussin," and so forth. When he is addressed as Tex by other characters in the story and is functioning as narrator of events, Vernon-Wood himself puts on a virtuoso linguistic performance, sending up hokey diction in every sentence, in a style reminiscent of Wodehouse's Bertie Wooster or Psmith.

In the end, Tex was no Grey Owl, nor was he anything like a colonial administrator, a conventional expatriate, or remittance man. He was a working man, ran a small business, and was an environmentalist to the extent that it squared with his living: guiding and hunting. In "It's Good to be Alive," Tex strikes a note of pragmatic frugality. Today, we might see this as environmentalist:

There's a heap of awful good chewin' on a Elk, an' when it comes to salvagin' meat, I'm a reg'lar Indian. Nothin' burns me up like the eggs who drop a prime animal, an' then just saw offen the head, an' leave the meat for the Coyotes an' Wolverines.

repeats the same idea in "Dried Spinach or Moose Steak?":

While I'm in line with a reasonable amount of conservation, an dead agin killin just to see a beast fall over, I'm also one of the old reactionaries who still figger that game was put in the mountains to provide huntin for men, an mebbe the odd woman.

And what of women in the wilderness? What did Tex make of them? In "Sawback Changes His Mind," Tex relates a successful hunting trip with the new wife of a long-time client, the Doc. Their initial fear that her presence will ruin a happy hunting trip proves groundless as she turns out to be "reg'lar," both to Tex and to his grizzled wrangler Sawback—meaning they accepted her as one of them because she was a good sport and a good hunter. Even in a less generous version of this story, "It's a Woman's World," the Doc's wife is caricatured as an outdoors-shy 'little woman' with scads of luggage, but she makes three magnificent kills without leaving camp, while Tex and her husband are hiking up and down mountains without success. In "Tex: Gentleman's Gentleman," he makes fun of dandies, comparing them unfavourably to female clients:

Instead of splashin' through the crick, which is all of four inches deep, he wanders up & down the bank lookin' for a log to cross on. When he found one, he got halfway across an' fell off. His mackinaw britches are all of a half inch thick, but there's a

Camp in winter

cupful of water splashed on 'em, so he returns to camp to break out another pair, an' that finishes that hunt. An' I've guided female women who've jumped into a glacier-fed crick up to their shirt pockets to bring a trout to net!

In "This Guiding Game," a reflection on different types of clients, we read:

It's funny about the women. Nine out of ten men ask, 'Isn't this trail thing too strenuous and rough for ladies?' I don't know if it's just luck, but any women I have had to do with fitted in like a cartridge in a rifle. I figure that if a woman don't like the outdoors she never gets far enough to get here. The ones that do, know they are going to like it, and that's half the battle.

The rest of that story is about a trip with a woman and her four daughters after the father of the family goes back to town, and Tex's admiration for all of them comes through loud and clear, especially for the eldest daughter, who out-shot him hunting in the mountains. An echo of this opinion appears in the 1969 interview with Maryalice Stewart, when Tex said of Mary Walcott's daughter "she was as good as any man I ever knew when it came to scrambling around in the hills."[39] Tex was no misogynist, as these stories and other remarks about him (cf. his first encounter with Mary Vaux Walcott, above) suggest; he felt women who could hunt and climb and fish had every right and reason to do so, and that was not exactly conventional.

There is little about religion in these stories: Tex was no church-goer. However, he repeatedly, when tired or frustrated due to bad luck or bad weather, regrets that he did not become a minister instead of a guide—though this is clearly not because of a high opinion of the ministry, whose sedentary and spiritual pursuits prevented them from living up to Tex's standards of mountain masculinity. In "Us Winter Sports," he makes light fun of the Methodist Church in Banff and of its minister, dubbed "Rev. Hackleberry," who did not predict winter sports in the afterlife for Tex and his friends. Yet in "The Guide Knows Everything," a priest gets top billing: Father Moriarty, who ran the Bankhead Mission, was an expert fly-fisherman, and thus fulfils a primary requisite of mountain masculinity, namely hunting or fishing prowess. The tender tone demonstrates that mountain masculinity did not have to be about filth and blood alone; friendship and ethical qualities and practices were also important.

39. Taped interview, S1/17 A, 22.

On the trail, 1924

I got so I invented jobs over to Bankhead on the off chance of runnin' into Father Moriarty an' persuadin' him to play hookey. I've seen him catch trout where there wasn't any, an' I never seen him lift more'n two out of the water in any one day. He'd bring 'em to the shallows, slip his fingers down the line an' takin' care his hand was wet, slip out his hook gentle as a woman. "There you are," he'd say. "Back to your pet eddy, an' meditate on the sin of gluttony, an' next time, don't mistake the shadow for the substance.

They buried the Father last fall. From the cemetery here, you can hear the Bow Falls roarin' loud an' deep in the spring, an' sort of musical the rest of the time, so his body is right handy to good trout water, an' I'll bet you four fits that his spirit is havin' one whale of a time with them other sportsmen, the Galilee fishermen, Ike Walton, an' Grey of Falloden."

Here again, Tex takes up the ideas of "muscular Christianity" of the late nineteenth and early twentieth centuries, which held that God had made men physically strong in order to bring social equality and justice to all. Tex's approval of religion that dovetailed with outdoor skills and his gentle contempt for anyone who did not think that physical pursuits and sporting activities in the great outdoors were the best pursuits of all is part of a long story about the need for strong, masculine English men to work hard on the frontiers of the British Empire.[40]

Tex did not fit neatly into our categories—he simultaneously inhabited different worlds that were at the time mutually exclusive, at least by convention; perhaps he was able to do so because frontier/colonial situations were sometimes inhabitable by people who did not fit into conventional class and gender roles in mainstream society in the first half of the twentieth century. He had definite ideas about proper sportsmanship and its proper articulation in nature and with nature, particularly in the mountains. These ideas had something of Baden-Powell's scouting ethos in them and something of traditional British country sportsmanship, but they are of further interest because they were elastic enough to accommodate women—especially the "New Woman" of the early part of the century who did not mind being outdoors and who, in the spirit of Mary Vaux and her friend, the Rocky Mountains traveller and explorer Mary Schäffer, didn't mind roughing it in the process with British-born guides to help them.

Tex's beliefs about women therefore, were not merely ad hoc, but programmatic, held on principle. It might be objected that Tex simply required a woman to "act like a man" in order to accept her, but there

40. See Coleman, 133–138.

was more to his ideal than that: many men, including accomplished athletes and anyone who just stuck around town in Banff and missed out on experiencing "the outdoors," fell short of the mark. He was himself a slender, bookish-looking fellow who wore little wire-rimmed spectacles, and thus by his own admission, was no lumberjackish heavyweight. Admission to the inner circle depended more on sportsmanship, fair play, respect for animals, lack of pretension, a willingness to sweat, get hot, wet, tired, and dirty, and a taste for hunting or fishing, than on a person's sex or physical characteristics—an intriguing mix of genteel Old World sportsmanship and vigorous New World egalitarianism.

Adventurer, guide, former British gentleman turned outdoors writer: Nello "Tex" Vernon-Wood isn't "CanLit" by a long shot. Why read these stories, then? The answer for us is that Tex lived during a pivotal time in the development of the Canadian Rockies from rough wilderness to national park system, and his writing shows us what a certain kind of masculinity—invented for his life in the mountains and for his readers—looked like. Tex's version of how a man should live and work in the outdoors has vanished along with the guided hunting and fishing industry that he helped to foster, but the lure of the mountains and the myth of the Canadian West as the place where identity can be remade is still a powerful one for the tourists and adventurers who visit the national parks. Tex Vernon-Wood was there before us, and his writing has much to tell us about what it was like to make a living in the great outdoors, and what kind of man he became in order to do it.

Andrew Gow
Julie Rak
Edmonton, 20 November, 2007

ONE

FIFTH AVENUE PILGRIMS AMID THE GOATS

This account, written as a letter from "Tex" to a friend, draws a clear line between real hunters and outdoorsmen who might smoke and be thin as a rail, but who can walk up and down mountains all day, and university graduates from fancy schools with degrees and athletic achievements but no sense of outdoorsmanship. Authenticity, class, education, masculinity, and bodies all matter very much here. Tex strongly identified himself as the former, and clearly found the poseurs he sometimes had to guide very tedious. One gets the sense that he was sometimes treated rather cavalierly by customers because he was a working man for hire, and not "one of them." Rather than complain about it, he found a way to make them look as foolish as they were—in stories such as this one. A young Ivy Leaguer eager for a chance to shoot a grizzly declines, when they finally find one, because he would have to cross a stream and get his feet wet, which he refuses to do. The story ends with Tex contemplating how he might even prefer the effete and pointless work (at least for a mountain man) of driving a bus to guiding this sort of customer. The question of authenticity is addressed clearly here: a man who can hunt and take care of himself in the mountains is a real man. People with money and fancy degrees from fancy schools start this game at a disadvantage. Supposed athletic prowess also knocks points off. Mockery directed at a guide with a thin body (of which he even makes fun himself) only makes the mocker look silly. The hunter's refusal even to cross a stream and get wet is the final nail in the coffin of his masculinity—the guide retreats in disgust. This is an odd mixture of machismo and a kind of anti-establishment counterculture sensibility, characteristic of the place betwixt and between inhabited by Tex.

—*AG and JR*

Fifth Avenue Pilgrims
Amid the Goats

———————— • ————————

A letter from a disillusioned guide
By N. Vernon-Wood

DEAR FRIEND:
I promised you when you were up here fishing last summer that I would let
you know how we came out with the hunting this fall.

Well, we had quite some hunt. Our three pilgrims were all from New
York, and when we met them at Lake Louise, to pull for the hunting
country on the Saskatchewan River, they looked just about the usual run
of the mill. Two middle-aged birds and a young feller. The king-pin of the
bunch was a large man name of Fogg. The other elderly man was sort of
quiet and didn't seem any too husky, and the young buck was John Julius
O'Toole, just out of Yale or Harvard or some one of those seats of learning
Down East.

I had started Frank ahead with the pack train, to make camp as far up
the Bow as we could make that day, so as soon as I had packed our pilgrims'
war bags and rifles we hit out up the trail. There wasn't much conversing
done, just the usual line about, "How far is it to camp?" and "What are
the prospects for a grizzly?" John Julius was just busting to tangle with a
grizzly. You know how it is the first day or so, the pilgrims are sort of sizing
up us fellers, and we are not missing anything that will give us a line on the
folks that we have to guide, council, and herd for the next month or so.

We caught up with the boys along about four o'clock, and as soon as we had ourselves sort of organized, the pot wrangler hollered, "Come and get it."

Then we did what was to do, to make camp snug for the night, and lay around the camp fire, sort of getting the feel of each other.

Suddenly, John Julius pointed his finger at me, like it was a gun, and said, "Wood, you smoke."

"Shure I smoke," I said.

"You smoke continually.

"Uh, uh," I replied.

"Well, you can't smoke like you do, and climb."

"Maybe I can't, but I never seen the pilgrim yet I can't keep two jumps ahead of," I come back. It's kind of one of the things you don't do, telling a mountain man he can't climb, especially before you have been out with him; but if you learn anything in this guiding game, it's the gift of patience with your fellow man.

Mr. Fogg says, "You men will have to look out for John, when you hunt with him. He is an athalete, and has got medals for the track and swimming and throwing the skillet," or words to that effect.

When we guides got into our tepee that night we did some mild arguing as to which of us were going to hunt with John, and which with the others. John looked good to all of us, and we all wanted him. You know how it is, each of us wanted to be the bird that got the most game. Well, to make it all according to Hoyle, we drew for them, and Frank got John, Jim gets Fogg, and me, with my usual luck, gets the little old fellow, whose name I find out is Boyle. To my mind he's the cull of the herd.

We got out of the park and into goat country on the third day out, and got all set to give the old billies a going over the next morning. Frank took a nice-looking draw east of camp, and I picked a long, grassy slope that was easy climbing, more with the notion of exercising my man than with getting any game. I always like to sort of break them in before I start to do any real hunting. I don't care how good shape a man keeps himself in in the city, 6,000 feet altitude and using new muscles takes the starch out, for a day or two, until you sort of get climated.

However, after poking along, onward and upward, for two three hours, darned if we didn't spot a bunch of goat sunning themselves on some ledges, about half a mile off. There was a steep shale slide behind them, which ran up to a cliff that was pretty straight up and down, and we were lucky to have the wind on them. There was a dry wash that ran up to the cliff, where the snow water had run off in the spring, and we could keep out of sight in that until we were close. The goat were plumb unsuspecting, and I figured everything was about as if I had ordered it.

We took lots of time, and when we finally poked our noses over the edge of the wash we were in a good position to start the massacre. I had Mr. Boyle rest him up a bit, so that the old heart wasn't pumping so hard that the muzzle of his rifle made circles, picked out a good-looking head, and give the word to plaster him. At the range we were, it should have been pie, but as the guy once said, "What a lot of country there is over and under and on both sides of a goat." One good thing about goat, they fancy themselves a heap, and shure believe it's no sign of a gentleman to be in a hurry. They will move off very deliberate as a general thing.

After the old boy had taken a couple of sighting shots, and put another down the foul line, he hit the billy a little low, but enough to make him sick. All this time the bunch were walking up the shale, looming up like a lighthouse in a fog. Finally, my man dropped enough lead into the goat to make him so plumb heavy that he couldn't climb any more, so he rolled over and called it a day. He had a nice head, too, and I skinned him out, made a pack of the head and scalp, with the liver for breakfast, and we started down, feeling pretty stuck on ourselves. Me, because I hadn't expected to get anything that day, only I didn't tell Boyle that.

We got into camp first, and after the cook had filled us up with honest-to-God trail tea, we lay around waiting for the rest to come in, so we could start lying about the long shots we had made, and the straight-up climbing we had done.

After a while along comes Frank with John Julius, and John is all he had with him, except a fair-sized grouch. Then Jim comes in, also traveling light. Frank had seen game but couldn't get a shot, he said, and Jim hadn't seen anything but tracks.

When we got into our tepee that evening, Frank opened up, and to hear him tell it John wouldn't ever get any medals for hunting. Frank told me that if I wanted John I could shure have him. I sort of figured that John had rubbed Frank against the fur, and that no man could be quite as useless as he made out John was, so I traded pilgrims.

Now, it was my notion to lay in this camp for a few days, so that the bunch could climb around and razz the goat, and this would put them in good shape for when we got into the sheep country. Anyone that can put one foot in front of the other for a few hours, and shoot reasonably straight, can get him a goat in this man's country, but the bighorn is a different breed of cat. He is no man's fool, and when you have accumulated you a good sheep head, you can swell out your chest and tell the world that you have done some real hunting. For this reason I like to blood my pilgrims on the goat before I hunt sheep with them. Then you have got 'em where they will stay with you all day, and shoot when the time comes. *Ovis Canadensis* doesn't wait around to see what you are going to do about it, and if you don't connect with him right smart, he goes from here to there awful pronto.

When we got up next morning, though, our pilgrims had had a powwow of their own, and wanted to break camp and hit for the sheep country right away. Nothing I could tell them seemed to cut any ice, and as they were paying for the outfit I gave in.

We chased the wrangler out after the ponies, broke camp, and lit out for the Wilcox Pass, about three days from where we were on the Mistaya. On the way, John kept pestering about grizzly. Man, oh, man, he shure wanted to tangle with one. I told him that if we did it was more luck than judgement, as at that time of the year, they were traveling all over the country. They keep mostly to the summits, digging gophers, filling up on them before they shut up shop for the winter.

Well, we got to the head of the Sunwapta and went into camp to look into the sheep proposition. Next day we hunted sheep, and the next, and the next.

Then one night it snowed about two inches. Just right for tracking. John and I started out bright and early and hit up a long slope heading for the alpine meadows on top. We were just about topping out when we ran into the finest set of grizzly tracks you would want to see. Fresh and hot, and by the look of them he wasn't in any hurry. He was angling down the hill on the north side toward a little pocket.

"Well, John, this is where you bust a bear," I said, and we followed the sign, keeping a peeled eye on the country below us. Finally, we come to the little pocket, which has scrub growing about three four feet high, and a creek running along the edge. The bear had crossed so soon ahead of us that the mud was still swirling around in his pads.

I told John to pump a shell into the chamber of his fowling piece and look at his sights, and sneaked across the stream as quietly as I could.

The water was just over my shoe tops. You know I wear usual height shoes. I think those high-legged ones are just so much more weight to pick up and put down. John has the kind sold at all the sportsmen's outfitters, seventeen inches high, anyway.

When I got to the other side, I find that John is still on the far bank, so I go back to find out how come. I didn't dare to holler for fear of disturbing our bear.

"Isn't there some kind of bridge I can cross on?" says he.

"Bridge, my foot, come on: the bear waded, and I waded, and neither one of us got drowned."

"No, I can't. You see, Wood, if I get my feet wet, my whole day will be spoiled."

Can you beat it? I told him to get the hell out of there and go back to camp, and by the nine blind pack ponies of old Joe Smith, that's just what he did.

I went back over the creek again, and followed the tracks, and about five-hundred yards into the bush here was the bear, busy as all get out, digging him some gophers.

I circled around him and hit for the camp myself. One more outfit like this, and I am going to quit and me a job chauffering one of those sight-seeing busses, from Calgary to Lake Louise.

"TEX."

The Sportsman, February 1930, 63 and 102

TWO

THIS GUIDING GAME

It turns out that some of the best mountain men are in fact women and girls. Tex was delighted by any client's ability to shake off city behaviour, as in the first episode, in favour of rugged mountain masculinity, and his delight was not limited by (though it was certainly shaped by) conventions about gender. When an anxious and haughty family father turns back to town and the nearest stock ticker after a few days on the trail, his wife and four daughters turn out to be excellent mountain men, fulfilling all the requisites of the mountaineering hunting ethos, from pranks right down to excellent shooting. Tex's mountain masculinity is, therefore, of an especially broad and comprehensive sort, connected not primarily to sexed bodies but more to gendered behaviour (or rather, in this case, to cross-gendered behaviour). As in other cases, Tex combines a type of outdoorsmanly machismo with a counter-cultural willingness to accept transgressions of convention, in this case gender-bending, and even to revel in them. Only the know-it-all professor comes off as irredeemable; even though he comes around to Tex's view of fires in teepees, he makes it out to have been his own idea—hardly a surprise in an academic.

—AG

This Guiding Game

———————— • ————————

Yarns of the wilderness by a competent outdoorsman
By N. Vernon-Wood

A LOT OF PEOPLE ASK ME why I stay with this guiding game when there's more money to be made at forty-seven other varieties of honest toil. I suppose the main reason is that I don't know anything else, and twenty years of ramming around the hills sort of gets under your hide and plumb ruins a man for punching a time clock. Then there's the kick a man gets out of his pilgrims; you get closer to a man in a month's camping than you will in ten years in an office. It's right interesting to start out with a flock of folks that you don't know the first thing about and watch how they shake down.

I get a letter from some bird in New York asking can I take him out for a month; and after we have made the usual business arrangements, he will most always write about what outfit he needs to bring. In the old days, this wasn't much to worry about, but since the "Blazed Trail has crossed the Boulevard," as the catalog says, life has gotten some complicated. I like to kid myself that I can get a sort of line on my prospects from these letters, but you can't always sometimes tell.

I hooked me a man one time for hunting bighorn. He made his arrangements in two telegrams, and I said to Jim, "That's the way we like 'em: short and sweet"; but old Bill Wilson that runs the post office here come pretty near asking Ottawa for a new office and more help before we got out on the trail. I got letters about beds, rifles, ammunition, field glasses, and clothes. He wanted to know if I could run a movie camera. Was my help congenial? I showed Jim that one, and it darn near cost me $10

47

a month. "If I have to be congenial after walking four–five miles through wet snow before breakfast wrangling your this and that pack r, it's going to cost you money, feller."

I got a letter saying that the Trans-Canada would land him at Lake Louise at ten forty-five in the morning, and that he would change into his trail clothes on the train and be ready to start at eleven. The day before he was due, I got a wire: "Bring plenty of strawberry jam." As I had sent the grubstake by freight and the rest of the outfit by trail two days ahead to Lake Louise, I had to chuck out some of my extra socks and shirts and stuff a few extra cans of jam in my war bag.

I was all primed to put in a month with one of those "Do it now," high-pressure ginks, and who was pernickety as the devil. I met him at the train, and I could see he was strung as tight as a fiddlestring and rarin to go. The outfit was camped across the tracks from the depot, and after we had collected his dunnage, we humped on over. Then Joe, the cook, broke the glad tidings that there wasn't any baking powder in the grubstake.

There's a sort of store three miles up the hill from the railway, and the only thing to do was grab a saddle pony and high tail up there. I told my dude he had better come too, and see the lake, anyway, as we would not come back that way, and Lake Louise is worth any man's time to see. I knew that he was figuring that I wasn't much of an outfitter, but I was certain I had ordered the baking powder, so I didn't worry much. The pilgrim unlimbered a box and got out a small movie camera, and away we went. While I went to see how much baking powder I could talk out of Casey Oliver up at the store, my man wandered down to the lake and it did look good that day. I darn near had to rope him and drag him away, and if he hadn't run out of film, we would have been there yet.

We didn't get away that day, and he said he wouldn't have missed it for a farm. All that was wrong with that guy was nerves. He had about worked himself to a frazzle and after he had slept out a few nights and done some climbing, he was right as rain. Instead of staying out a month, he ran it nearly two, and we were down to straight sheep meat and bannock, but it was jake with him. Jim and Joe kicked like bay steers because we were out of jam and sweet stuff, but our pilgrim didn't let out a word. He was a contented as a hog in mud, and as long as there was game to stalk, he would stay on a mountain all day and night. Around camp he was one of the gang, and we all liked him plenty, which just proves you can't look at a frog and figure how far he will jump.

I got stuck with a bunch of scientific sharps once that nearly got my nanny, though. Most any pilgrim will give a guide credit for knowing something, but these birds allowed we were just about one short jump ahead of a pack horse in intelligence. The big augur of the layout was a professor of geology, and he was highbrow and high-hat. He had a dinky hen-skin sleeping bag that didn't look very adequate to me, so I figured that I would put him in the tepee with me and his assistant, and keep a fire going lots when we got up higher.

When he saw me packing a load of nice dry jack pine into the tepee that night, he wanted to know what for. I explained about his bag, and said I would see that the fire was kept going. You should have heard him blow up. He had gotten that bag out of a book on camping, and it was the last work in lightness and comfort, and anyway who ever heard of a fire inside a tent. Preposterous and unthinkable, and a lot more. Besides, his bed would likely catch fire. I offered to bet him four bits that when he got through he would burn it, anyhow, but he wouldn't take advantage of my abysmal ignorance. Then I tried to tell him the difference between a tepee and a tent, and explained that the Indians had been using them for some considerable time, and that they cooked in 'em and everything, but it was no go. He just naturally knew that you couldn't have a fire inside a canvas thing without having it flaming round your ears, so I let it go at that. We had to camp up on the Pipestone Pass for him to get some geology, and it was crimpy round the edges up there. I used to get a heap of satisfaction lying in my snoozing sack and list'ning to the professor shivering himself warm and using what I figured was academic cuss words.

One evening he sort of circled around to the subject of fires in tepees, and I lit a small one that night. He watched it carefully for quite a while, and then started to give his assistant and me the scientific principles involved, why the smoke, etc., went out of the vent, and before a week went by, to hear him tell it, he was the bird that invented tepees, and he had figured some improvements that the Nitchies had overlooked.

A couple of nights after, we were sitting round the camp fire, smoking and telling lies, when Jim says: "I struck a fossil bed up that creek across from camp when I went after the horses this morning. There's a bench of Cambrian rock there plumb full of trilobites; look-it this one." I saw the professor sort of prick up his ears, and, knowing Jim was kind of hipped on geology, I says, "I thought it was igneous rock up there." "Igneous my foot," says Jim. "You know damn well that the only igneous rock in this part is in the Ice River Valley; this is all sedimentary," and away he goes ridin' his hobby to a queen's taste. He started at the Pre-Cambrian and went all the way up and down the line. You could have knocked the professor's eyes off with a club, they boggled out so.

When we got to our tepee for the night, he said, "I had no conception, Wood, that you men knew any geology. That man's discourse this evening was most interesting and authoritative." "Hell," I said, "we travel with so many brainy sharps, and have to listen to 'em, that we get so we can discourse on anything from gin to geology, and half the time we don't know what we are talking about ourselves."

Then there is the chap that wants to see the whole of the Rocky Mountains in ten days. He most always comes up provided with all the maps that he can accumulate, and expects to go through the country on the high lope. There used to be a New Yorker and his wife that came here every summer, and they got so they were sure stuck on this neck of the woods, but I had to educate him to the right way to enjoy it. The first trip he made, he sort of had the notion he wasn't getting his money's worth because a day's travel only got him about fifteen miles or so from where he had started. He didn't figure that you can't chase pack horses without laying up a bunch of grief. If you get two miles and a half an hour out of a string you are doing about average, and five hours of that is a day's work for a horse that has to rustle his living. You can't rush, and not have sore backs and poor horses.

Every evening the judge would get out his map and have me show him exactly where we were. Then he would point two–three inches farther on, and ask, "Can't we get here tomorrow?" I tried to explain the difference between a few inches of trail on paper and the stuff we had to herd the outfit over. The maps do not show all the kinks and twists on the trail, or put in the windfalls that have to be cut, or the muskeg that bogs the ponies. Neither do they show where there's horse feed and where there ain't a thing but spruce forest, so that you have to suit your day's travel to your camping places. It all looks smooth as frog hair on the maps.

Well, we have to send our pilgrims home satisfied, if we expect to make a living, so we aims to please. I laid low until we had been out long enough for the grub packs to get lightened some and we had made the turn for home. Then one morning we shook ourselves out bright and early and gave an imitation of three guides breaking camp on the jump. I told the judge that we would camp at Bow Lakes that night, which was all of thirty miles from where we were on the Saskatchewan. I took good care not to tell him that last part, though.

Joe gave all hands a couple of dough gods and some cold bacon to put in our saddle pockets, and we were away with a whoop and a holler. We lost a little time cutting out windfalls on Bear Creek, and a fool pony bogged down on those mud slides at the foot of the Pyramid, but outside of that we plugged along steady as you please. It was getting dusk when we went over Bow Pass, and by the time we had dropped down below the lakes it was dark as the insides of a black cat.

We didn't have any company around the camp fire that night; the judge had been kind of quiet for the last few hours. Next morning he didn't show up when Joe yelled, "Grub pile," so I went to his tent to see how come.

He just opened one eye and says, I think we had better lay over today, Wood."

I thought so, too. He was so stiff his eyelid creaked when he opened it. His wife and I went fishing, but he didn't show up until long about four o'clock in the afternoon. He was back the next summer, and while we were sort of going over things before we hit the trail, he said, "I just want to loaf around this trip, Wood. I think there is something in what you say about the disadvantage of rushing through the country." Just then I caught his wife's eye, and I had to look hard at his fishing rod.

It's funny about the women. Nine out of ten men ask, "Isn't this trail thing too strenuous and rough for ladies? I don't know if it's just luck, but any women I have had to do with fitted in like a cartridge in a rifle. I figure that if a woman don't like the outdoors she never gets far enough to get here. The ones that do, know they are going to like it, and that's half the battle.

One summer we got a family that had me worried for a while. There was Mr. and Mrs. Van Dieman, three daughters, and a governess. Five females, and we figured that they would have us herding with the squirrels before they got through. Old man Van was sort of stuck on himself, and didn't approve of his family getting too friendly with any rough-neck horse wranglers. I heard him bawling out the youngest one day because she came over to where we were talking about this and that, and it sort of got me on the prod. We hadn't been out only two days when he got to ghost dancing about what the market was doing, and said he would have to go back.

I started Jim back with him, feeling sort as if I had fallen down on my job, and that the market was just a bluff, but Mrs. Van called me over, and said, "Now, don't feel badly about this, Tex. My husband really hates camping and has never finished any trip we have started. I think possibly that we will get along quite well without him."

"You're happy right," thinks I, but kept it at thinking.

Fifteen minutes after Jim and old Van had left camp you could feel the difference. While we lay in camp waiting for Jim to get back, we climbed and fished and had a sort of field day. I want to tell the world, that after I had put in a day with that aggregation on a mountain, I knew I had been some place. There wasn't a thing they wouldn't try once. Every morning they would line up in bathing suits and hit the Spray River. Man, I used to be scared pink. The water was swift and cold as charity, but as Joe said, "All them gals need is gills, and they would sure be fish." They were right sore because I wouldn't let 'em ride a bronc we were trying to break for a pack horse. Us guides never knew the minute one of 'em wouldn't pull some stunt on us that would trip us into the drink, or such like. We would find our sleeping bags sewn up, and one rainy night they let our tent down on us.

They showed Joe a thing or two about cooking, and did it so that he didn't get peeved about it; and by the red-eyed Mike, the oldest one beat the skin off me at shooting. The day we got back to Banff they gave us a party up at the big hotel, and danced us bow-legged. Someone asked me if women weren't quite a problem on the trail. I'll tell a man they are, but not the way that bird meant.

The Sportsman, April 1930, 58–59 and 78

THREE

THE LAST GREAT BUFFALO DRIVE

Tex relates a number of past film experiences in this story, though not the months he and his family spent in California, when he worked in Hollywood as an animal handler, notably on *The Call of the Wild*. From raucous by-play during the shooting of a silent movie and mockery of the Alpine folk costumes (lederhosen in particular) featured in the film through a well-deserved but painful assault on the backside of a pain-in-the-ass assistant director with home-made buckshot, the atmosphere rings true to anyone who has ever had the misfortune to hang around a movie set as an extra or a relative. Tex clearly spent a good deal of time working on movies. His mockery of what directors thought looked real vs. reality is especially fresh and apt. Both the buckshot episode and the unintended killing of a buffalo, then a rare animal in Canada, were, if true, very masculine hi-jinks and would lead to much more serious consequences today. The rough-and-tumble of those days is one point of this story, with the implicit message that one could no longer get away with such macho goings-on (for better or for worse, with the decision left to the reader).

—AG

THE LAST GREAT BUFFALO DRIVE

———— • ————

When the simple sons of nature make history
in true Hollywood fashion
By N. Vernon-Wood

JIM BROUGHT OUT A FLOCK of magazines, last time he went in for the mail, and there was some of those moving picture periodicals amongst 'em. They got me to thinking about some of our experiences with the actors and actorines. For a while there was quite a run on these hills for background for he-man stuff.

The first outfit we got tangled up with blew into Lake Louise, it must be all of eighteen years ago, and they were taking a play that was supposed to take place in Switzerland. Our old log bunk house was all dolled up, to represent a Swiss châlet, and a bunch of the village bums were dressed up in those dinky pants that show all the spavins on an old man's legs, and those Hamburg hats, with tail feathers. It's a good thing this was before the days of talkies because us horse jinglers used to gather on the side line and kid the troops. You should have seen old Pop Denton, in Boy Scout pants, with his galluses all embroidered, and with half a snoot full, atmosphering. When the bunch got to razzing him, the atmosphere was there all right. Blue, mostly it was.

The main squeeze was a little man with a bumper crop of hair. I bet it would of harvested 100 ton to the acre, and we called him Henry Irving,

---

This story was reprinted in an Alberta school anthology: Theresa M. Ford, ed., *Western Moods* (Edmonton, AB: Alberta Education, 1979), 30–36, as an example of humorous Alberta writing.

right away. What he lacked in beef he made up in words and hair. To hear him, you would have thought that he made the blue prints for the Creator. I found out that since that that's the way a lot of those movie directors feel about themselves.

Tom Gordon was wrangling for me those days. He had gotten into an argument in Nevada, and was sort of vacationing until his opponent either died or didn't. Good man, any place you put him, and one of the kind that women turn round to get another look at, but I don't think he knew it, or would have bothered if he did. There was a bit of a girl in the movie party that did the stunts for the leading lady, and she and Tom got right friendly. She didn't seem to to rate very highly with the beauties or Henry, but she was more our kind, and had enough nerve for the bunch and then some.

The story called for the star to be shoved into a crevasse by the villain, then her faithful old hound hits for the village and does his stuff, so that the hero goes back on to the ice with him and pulls the usual rescue. Tom and I packed the cameras and the props up to the Victoria Glacier, and hunted up a crevasse that filled the bill. We had a bunch of old mattresses which we piled in the bottom, where it was about twenty feet deep, and Tom's lady friend is elected to be heaved in. The cameras were all sighted, and Henry gave a lecture on how he wanted it done. Then the girl and the villain put up a battle on the edge, and in she went. It looked like million dollars to us, but Henry says, "Rotten." They do it again, and Henry's verdict is "Rottener if possible." He called the girl down some, and ordered another. The third time he grabbed a double handful of his hair and started to tell the world his private and personal opinions of stunt girls. He got so hopped up, he used the wrong word once. It isn't anymore than out of his face, when Tom shoved it back. When the birdies quit singing for Henry, he sort of looked around and wanted to know if the avalanche had killed many. After he had recovered fully, he opined that the picture would do, so we went back to the châlet. If he could have got another pair of pack-horse artists we would have gone down the road the hay come up, talking to ourselves.

Our next splash into the realms of art come near getting us a position making big ones into little ones for His Majesty. The Government used to keep a heard of buffalo in a big pasture just outside the town for tourists and schoolmarms to look at. This was before the Pablo herd was bought and shipped up from Montana and a bison was worth more than ten men. Every year the Stonie Indians camp just outside the pasture, when they pull their annual celebration. They were there the time this happened, and their camp sure looked slick with the tepees all painted up, and the bucks in their best beads and feathers.

Jim, Buckshot Foster, and me, with two or three more foot-loose ginks , were in the Birdcage, finding out if Johnny Walker was still going strong, when a bird come over where we were at, and said he was willing to pay for another investigation. He told us that him and his partner were taking movies of the mountains and what not, and that he had tried to get the Indians to let him take some camp stuff and the like, but he wasn't successful. "They won't even talk English," he said.

"They don't talk to strangers, and they sure won't let you take photos if you don't sweeten them up," Buckshot told him. I guess the last investigation had made Buckshot kind of good natured, because he offered to go down to the camp with our visitor, and fix things up for him. Having nothing on our minds, Jim and I went along too. Just as we got to the pasture, a bunch of buffalo came tearin' down out of an aspen grove and round the flat.

"What a sight," says our fillum expert. "Boys, I've just had a brain wave, here's a herd of buffalo, and also a bunch of Indians. Do you think it would be possible to stage a buffalo hunt? If you can persuade those Indians to ride into the pasture, all done up in paint and feathers, and pretend to shoot the animals with their bows and arrows, I will buy enough Johnny Walker for you to continue your scientific researches for a week."

Foster figured he could work the Nitchies all right, but wasn't sure how old Adam Galletly, who was caretaker of the herd, would take to the idea.

"You give me a crock of Johnny, as a retainin' fee, and I will reason with Adam," I offered, so we went back to the Birdcage, and had a conference, same as all movie magnets do, and after a while Buck and I started out to arrange our bigger and better production.

It took three quarters of the retaining fee to convince Adam that we weren't up to some deevilment , as he put it. "Ye have tae do it early tomorrow morn, and mind ye, if the soopreentendant hears aboot it, I ken naethin' o' it."

The Indians were not so easy; we couldn't use the same argument with them but finally, for $4.00 hard cash and a set of busted harness I owned, half a dozen agreed to star for us. We gave them the layout. Next morning we were to be in the field right soon, and we would gather the herd up in a draw that led out of the pasture. Then we would haze them down hell bent, and just as they come through the aspens, the warriors were to cut in behind, and try to ride up close enough to shoot a few arrows into the ground in front of or under the bulls.

It worked like a charm. We got about twenty bulls coming down that draw like the milltails of hell, and the braves cut in, yelling and coyoteing, feathers streaming and everything just like the story books. The excitement got too much for old Chief Running Horse. I guess the crazy old devil had killed buffalo just this way in his youth, and his years fell off him, and he rode up to a bull, drew his bow darn near double, and socked an arrow in right behind the shoulder, where it would do the most good. In about two jumps the animal gave a most ungodly plunge, turned end over end, and was as dead as King Rufus in two minutes.

"Red-eyed old Jeehosephat," said Foster. "here's where you and I head to Montana, with a price on our heads for incitin' war, rebellion, and killing the King's pet buffalo. Feller, if this gets out, you and I will be provided for, for the next ninety-nine years."

We gathered up our warriors, who were just as much scared as us, and told them that if that man Government and the Mounted Police got wise to our morning's work, the whole reservation would be shipped to Lethbridge, and put to work farming, besides being fined a million ponies. They just oozed out of that field and back to camp.

Our fellow criminals were so disorganized they wanted to bust up the film, but I said, "No, you birds get out of here, on the jump, and if Buckshot and I are hung for this, when you sell the picture of the 'Last Great Buffalo Drive,' see that our sorrowing friends get a supply of conversation water, to remember our virtues on. They will need plenty."

Two minutes later we were alone in the bloody field, and Buckshot wants to know whatinhell we are going to do about it. Me, I've been thinking fast, up, down, and in circles, and I explain, "Now, see here, this bull was gored, trampled to death by the rest of the herd, and although you and I did some fancy riding trying to rescue him, we failed. Help me get this blame arrow out of him, and roll him over." We did just that, then we get a club apiece, and went over the corpse, bumping off some hide here and there, and generally using him up. After that we hazed as many of the buffalo we could gather up in a hurry, and milled them around in the vicinity of the corpus delicti. I beat it for Adam's shack on the high lope, and told him to get a wiggle on and saddle his old hay burner, as the buffalo were on the prod, and fighting like Kilkenny cats.

He took time to get on the telephone and notify the Supe, and chief warden, and all the rest of His Majesty's representatives. By the time we were in the field, there is a peerade of officials as long as this yarn, streamin' out of town. Lucky for us the herd is still wooling around the flat, snorting, and throwing dust over their backs. The brains view the sad sight from a safe distance, and tell Adam to skin out the beast when the others have quieted down. We remained in the background, like the modest heroes we are, and tell Adam we will help him when he gets ready. We don't want that canny Scot to get on to the hole behind the shoulder if possible. The officials go back to the office, to start on their reports. "Regrettin' to state," and I head for the Birdcage to collect another retainer, so that when skinning time comes, Adam will be indisposed.

We laid off trying to contribute our mite to the cause of art for quite some time after that.

Our next personal appearance is not quite so exciting for us, but that doesn't make us mad. A company from one of the big studios in Hollywood came up to make a Western thriller. It looked like they were God's gift to trail hands, as it had been a hard old winter, and those of us that weren't broke were badly bent, as is usual in the spring. Five big round dollars a day, with lunch thrown in for being half-breeds, cow-punchers, desperadoes, and otherwise acting about natural, sure listened like the answer to somebody's prayer.

First thing this outfit did was to build a whole village about twenty miles from town, and we all went to work getting out logs, and building shacks. They even imported a flock of hens to scratch around the village, and Jim and I used to figure on about nine eggs a day, until some more of the gang got on to our graft and we had to cut it out. They took us out every morning in cars, and brought us back at night, and somebody in the bunch had brains, because we got our $5 every day. Prosperity dawned, and the sun shone on both sides the fence. The only fly in the jam was the assistant director, and he was some fly. He kept a pony up at the location, and he galloped hither and yon, yelling orders so fast he had us poor benighted hill-billies all rattled. When he wasn't on the gallop, he sat on top of the cayuse surveying the scene. All he needed was a lick of gold paint to have done for that statue of General Lee that you see up Fifth Avenue as you get up by Central Park in the big city.

We felt kind of sorry for the poor little cayuse. That flying Dutchman was a heavy man, and he sure did make mileage. The bunch did a lot of figuring how we could help out the pony, but there didn't seem much we could do about it, until we heard one morning that everything was set to make a big fight scene. Every one of the atmosphere was issued with a

30.30 and all the blank ammunition he wanted. Right away about four of us had the same flicker of intelligence, and we straightened out the crimping at the end of the blanks. I happened to have a few of the real honest shells in my belt, so we pulled the bullet out of a couple, put a pinch or two of cordite out of them into our blanks, and then filled them with small stones, and anything that was hard and small. We made one or two wooden plugs about the same size as a 30.30 bullet, and then waited to see what would turn up.

The dope was, that the hero and his girl were in bad with the rough-necks, and we were besiegin' them in a shack at the end of the village. We were given a course on how we should stalk up to the shack and fire as we sneaked along, the loving couple in the meantime giving us all the hell they can.

The assistant didn't trust us simple sons of nature to stalk that shack in the true Hollywood fashion, so he mingled with the herd to give instructions, and then the signal went up to commence hostilities. We sure put up a wonderful lookin' scrap. Shoot, and crawl for the next bush or rock. Every once in a while, one of the defenders would drill an enemy, and he would clutch the wound and, laughing to fit to bust, die where the cameras would catch him.

Then through the smoke, I saw our hated enemy, bending down behind a rock, yelling at a breed to put more snap into it. I gave the tip to my fellow-desperadoes, and next minute he jumped forty feet in the air, clutching the seat of his riding breeches, and yelling bloody murder. I bet he was wounded in thirty-nine places. I do know that the pony got plenty rest after, as he done his galloping around on foot for quite a while.

Sometime, I think I will write to one of those movie magazines and spill some on screen shots of my own.

The Sportsman, June 1930, 75, 86 and 88

FOUR

"William, Prepare My Barth"

This story is the most clearly mocking of gentlemanly big-game hunters, and it happens also to be directed programmatically against Tex's former countrymen, the English (called "Woodbiners," in the slang of the day). The prejudice against Englishmen that Tex encountered when he arrived in Canada (cf. John Gow's recollections in Appendix A) was real; appended to "help wanted" signs in shop windows was often the coda "Englishmen Need not Apply." As exhibits at the museum in Fort Steele Heritage Town in British Columbia document, prejudice against the English middle- and upper-class settlers was particularly strong in the mountains of western Canada at that time because they were not seen as good settlers. Tex did a great deal to shed that stigma, though he never really shed important parts of his identity, such as his tea at 11:00, or subscribing to what was then still called the *Manchester Guardian* by air mail. But his desire to distance himself from the stereotype of his fellow countrymen means that Tex often presented himself as a real Canadian, unlike his English clients, who are just tourists.

This story demonstrates Tex's authentic Canadianness by emphasizing the effete and silly gentlemanliness of his clients. Again, mountain masculinity is at stake here: excessive bathing, attention to the body and clothing, and to comfort are clearly not proper masculine behaviours in the mountains. One has the sense that this is situational, and that Tex he would be perfectly happy for them to be fastidious English gentlemen at home and in private, just as he was a tea-drinker and *Guardian*-reader—at home and in private. But in his stories and out in the wilderness at least, as Tex he expected conformity to a masculine ideal of ruggedness and insouciance about comportment (washing and comfort) in the mountains—an expectation that he passed down to his children and grandchildren, much to AG's annoyance as a child. In "Pipestone Letter No. 1," Tex notes that most guides "generally expect a Pilgrim to be washing, shaving, and cleaning his nails, when he ought to be scrambling up a slide to try and bust a bear." Perhaps we can speak of situational norms of ethnic national and gender display—but the mocking description of the great hunters sitting in Morris chairs in the shade, waiting for beaters to drive a gazelle past their guns is too funny to be submitted to dry analysis alone—it is high satire and has its own raison d'être. The ending has a nice populist touch.

—AG and JR

"William, Prepare My Barth"

———————— • ————————

A big, thick catalogue has kept many a homesteader
in literature all winter
By N. Vernon-Wood

I GOT A FLOCK OF SPORTING goods catalogues last time I went in for the mail, and Jim and I have been beguiling the long winter evenings buying ourselves a real Fifth Avenue trail outfit. In our minds, I figure that for about $1500 I can just about get the bare necessities of life as it's lived out in the hills and woods, according to the catalogues above mentioned.

There's a lot of real useful dooflickers in the books, and a lot that remind me of old Bill Baxton's teeth. Bill's been up here ever since Mt. Assiniboine was a hole in the ground. He started out as a packer for the Hector survey, the one that layed out the C.P.R. line here in the 'eighties. Then he took to prospecting, and did some guiding too, but pilgrims were some scarce in those days. When the Boer War bust out, Bill was single jacking his way into the inside of the main range of the Selkirks, hoping to run down a vein that would assay just about $1000 to the pack-horse load, but quit to go to war in Africa with Strathcona's Horse.

When that fracas was settled, Bill came back, and did this and that, until the last W. K. war broke loose. By this time he was showing plenty of rings on his horns, but he got into a cavalry outfit and was sent to Calgary to train. The only thing wrong was that he didn't have what you call a full string of teeth, so the Army staked him to a new set of removable ones.

One of the boys went down to visit Bill, and found him sitting on the steps of a hut, whittling away on his store teeth with a skinning knife. He

63

would try them in his face, cuss a little, and take 'em out and go to hewing on them again.

"That's the devil of a way to use your teeth, Bill," says his visitor.

"Oh hell, these are for military purposes only. I spit 'em out before I eat," says Bill.

Just the same it beats everything what a kick a man can get out of a catalogue. A big, thick one from a mail-order house has kept many a trapper in literature all winter. I bet you that when a pilgrim is buying his first outfit for a hunt, he gets more kick out of it than if his U.S. Steel jumped ten points. It's surprising, too what a heap of whifflows a good salesman, that's never slept out in his life, can unload on to a hard-headed wolf on Wall Street, and it's more surprising how these same get lost, bust, or left in the last camp, when the guides get to handling them.

There was an outfit come up here once, that undertook to show the native hill-billies and the world in general just how it should be done. They spread the news that they were going where the foot of white man had never trod, and that's some contract, when you figure that the Hudson's Bay men were ramming around here 200 years ago, and that there must have been two Scotch prospectors in before them, not counting the ones that's been going up and down and across since. They had everything except a portable tennis court. It would have taken two men and a boy to see all their pack string at once, and I bet they would have had to take two looks at that. I followed them out about two weeks later, and if I had had time and also about ten extra pack ponies I could have accumulated enough stuff that was scattered over the trail to have issued a tricksy catalogue of my own.

When it comes to hitting the trails de lux, though, it takes an Englishman to do it up brown, with butter on both sides. I got me a brace of Woodbiners before the war, and they brought everything except the brick house. They had a chest of silver, and a valet to see that we didn't pinch the spoons, and to fill the bathtub. Their tents would hold a round-up crew and were as heavy as a green cook's bannock. The tents had telescope poles, with wooden hickeys to screw on top of the uprights, painted red, white, and blue. That was to show us bally Colonials where we got off at. Their rifles assayed $500 to the ton, and there was anyway $2,000 worth of them. We sure were some relieved when we finally got into hunting country so that all we had to do was about sixteen hours a day hunting and camp chores; some of the ponies were sway-backed from packing that layout.

As soon as we got through moving every day, those Englishmen began to live like the best County families do it. The minute the cook made a move in the morning, one or the other would holler, "William, prepare my barth." William was the valet, and he would hightail for the creek with two collapsible pails and fill the folding tub, in the portable bath tent. By the time an ordinary outfitter would have fed and got to hunting, they would be just about bathed and shaved. Old Stiggs, the cook, began to get infected too, and opined he would throw some dog, so he made him a white apron out of a flour sack. It was plumb ritzy, too, until one day he was reaching over the cook fire to move a pot of mulligan and his apron caught fire. When we got him extinguished he was shy a flock of whiskers and eyebrows, and that put a crimp into his dog.

I sure felt sorry for William, though. Those birds ran him bow-legged, and he was scared stiff that if he didn't hit her on the nose he would get the tin can tied to him and left in the Colonies to starve or get scalped by hostiles. When one of his bosses would holler, "William," the Wrangler would say, "Tell him to go plumb, Bill. Be a man and tell him to go take a jump in the lake." Bill would just about have a hemorrhage for fear one of the dukes would hear, and that didn't worry us any.

I had my grief too. I couldn't persuade those guys to hunt on foot. Their idea was to ride up to the game. "What's the use of barging around in the forest, when one can ride down the parths," was their notion. I've quit arguing with any pilgrim that wants to tell me how to hunt. The thing to do is give 'em their own way, until they see that it ain't putting any meat in the pot, or helping the taxidermists to earn an honest dollar. They will come around then and give my system a whirl.

They used to tell us yarns about hunting in India and Africa, where they had a million misguided heathens herd the game past a couple of Morris chairs, in the shade of the fig trees, and then they would take their rifle from the second assistant rifle wallah and plug the galloping gazelle as he fogged by. It kind of got Jim's nanny. He could see where he might have to get old Stiggs and herd a grizzly through camp while I stood by with a cup of tea and the extra 490 express.[1] So he says one day, "I hope to God you fellers don't think for one Jeezley minute you are in India now." "Oh, no," says one of the earls, "The vegetation is quite different." That took a load off of Jim's mind anyway.

There's a lick just where the Simpson and Vermillion come together,

1. A powerful hunting rifle.

and it's quite a stamping ground for moose, so we figured that our best bet to horseback our dudes to game was to get up before breakfast some morning and ride down there, and we might jump a moose that was late hitting back to the green timber for the day. We put this proposition to our pilgrims, and they thought that at last I was showing glimmerings of human intelligence. Next morning Jim got in the saddle horses about four o'clock, and we rolled out the valet and he did his stuff. Then the barons started to get ready to commence to begin. They bathed, shaved, massaged, and had a little tonic on their hair. About nine o'clock breakfast is disposed of, and they beat it for one of their rag houses, and went into conference to decide what rifle, knife, field glasses, etc., was the de rigger for that day. Long about ten o'clock William appeared, and says that if Mr. Stiggs would make a cup of tea, the gentlemen would be ready to proceed immediately after.

I could see that Wrangler of mine swelling up, and figured any minute he would blow up and bust. Old Greasy, though, is so ticked with the Mr. Stiggs stuff, that he got into motion, and started to distill his so-called tea. Then William picked the correct spoons from the perambulatin' safety vault, and packed the onsomble into one of the tents.

Just about then I got interested in an old Billy, about three miles away on a slide, and watched him through my glasses for quite a while. He seemed to have a bum leg, and was not as full of the old sangfroid as a goat generally is. Jim was fiddling around the ponies, and I didn't take much notice of what he was doing until I heard the ponies hitting up the trail for the rest of the herd. Before I could start to bawl him out he beat me to it, and asked me if it was in the price to let the cayuses stand all day tied to trees, when they had to rustle like hell to scratch a living in this so and so valley of mine anyhow.

I am just about to ask him when he got so full of loving-kindness to a flock of plugs that were only waiting a good chance to kick him in the diagram, when out come the lords, and says, "All right, Wood, Shall we proceed? Oh, I say, where are the mounts?" "Gone to get 'em a cup of tea, blast your armorial bearin's," hollered Jim, and that put the tin hat on that day.

Just the same, that had a heap of influence with the baronets, and we got on a whole lot better after. When they got down to earth as far as hunting was concerned, they couldn't be beat. Under their shells they were good sports and I like 'em, even if I did get mad enough to put coyote poison in their tea sometimes.

I often wonder what happened to William, though. The day we got back to Banff, we packed up our pilgrims' trophies, and then started up the village to give the bartenders a chance to justify their existence, and we run into Bill down on some errand for one of his marquises. We sort of herded him into our pet bar, and the last I saw of him, he was going up the street, toward the big hotel, and he was sure using a lot of the right way—both sides and the middle—and I heard him tell a mounted corporal, "I'm going up there, and I'm going to tell those bl-blighters, to take an extended sprint an' plunge into the water."

The Sportsman, July 1930, 55 and 78

FIVE

Us Winter Sports

This is the piece with the greatest immediate historical significance, as it suggests and describes an origin for the introduction of skiing to the Banff area. This new winter sport and the facilities it spawned radically changed Banff from the summer resort that it had remained until well into the middle years of the twentieth century: the Banff Springs Hotel and Chateau Lake Louise simply shut down in winter. Before that, wealthy tourists who arrived by sleeper car on the toney CPR Trans-Canada, a stainless-steel rhapsody of Art Deco design, took the hot mineral waters at the Cave and Basin, walked or went out hunting or fishing—in summer. Here, Tex comically refers to the founding of the Skoki Lodge by the Ski Club of the Canadian Rockies near Banff in 1931. Skoki Lodge was (and remains) a back-country skiing destination three years before Tex's first boss, Jim Brewster, made Sunshine Village into the first ski resort in the Rockies. Skiing turned Banff into a year-round tourist destination. Tex refers to the anonymous inventor as "some yahoo" who "got to ghost dancing," a reference to the ghost dance of the Plains Indians. The reference is apt: diverse Native groups adopted the ghost dance as a mystical way to bring back the buffalo herds and become prosperous once again, much as (in Tex's eyes) the Banff area was looking for more ways to bring in tourist dollars.

The popularization of the automobile and therefore of cheap mass travel made resort skiing wildly popular after the First and Second World Wars, but Tex's stories had all been written before that time—one can only imagine what he would have made of skiing day-trippers from Calgary and bus-loads of Japanese tourists. Tex's self-mockery about his clumsy and amateurish use of skis is a winning counterpoint to his slightly grudging appreciation of Cliff White's visionary introduction of skiing to the area.

69

His point about the money to be earned guiding or teaching skiers was in a minor way prophetic, as his own son and daughter-in-law (Bill and Choukie Vernon-Wood) would run a small ski-hill near Vernon, and his grandson John Gow would start out as a ski instructor at Sunshine Village and finish as its general manager, before taking over and building up, in partnership, Silver Star Resort near Vernon, thus mirroring Tex's own trajectory in the tourist business from Banff into British Columbia.

—*AG and JR*

Us Winter Sports

———— • ————

Some efforts in the Canadian Rockies to make San Moritz
look like a dirty deuce
By N. Vernon-Wood

Does beat hell how complicated life's getting up here in the hills. Take this pilgrim wrangling, fr'instance. Used to be, a man could bust out for a month on the trail, with a few plugs of spitting tobacco, and his other socks. As long as you had plenty sow belly, beans, flour, tea and sugar, with the odd fish hook, that's all anybody looked for. Try and get away with that now. We got to have grapefruit for breakfast, and a table to eat it off.

Last summer, I was guiding a party and, after Joe had set up for the first meal, they looked the layout over, some disdainful, and asked where was the butter knife and napkins. Seeing they was ladies, I couldn't tell 'em that we mostly used the seat of our Levi's for napkins.

A couple of years back, I built me a log cabin at Spray Lakes, figuring on making it the ritziest camp in Alberta. I packed out real windows, and a stove. Put down a lumber floor, and furnished it regardless, with cots and trick folding chairs. Then I spread myself, and spent real money advertising it. First reply I got was from a bird who asked, "What other attractions have you besides fishing, climbing, and hunting? Have you a tennis court?" Joe says that next summer we had better pack along a flock of putters and balls, so the dudes can play this pup golf in and out the teepees.

It's demoralizing the hands too. I hired a new jingler last spring, and the doo funnies that waddy wanted to pack would have sunk a scow. He even had a book.

In July, I had to go up to the big hotel, to talk to some folks about a hunting trip, and may I never throw another diamond hitch, if here ain't Buckshot Foster going into the dining room, with a party he had just brung in from the Saskatch, all rigged out in a soup and fish. He looked about as happy as a buckskin cayuse at the National Horse Show.

Up till this hectic stuff hit us, if a man knew the country, run a good spread of cayuses, and didn't get too awful grouchy when a pilgrim missed a easy shot at a head he'd taken plenty trouble to injun up on—why, that's about all anyone looked for. Now, you got to be a guide, scientist, conversation expert, and God knows what all, including, "How much exposure shall I give this?" Well, you can't stay in the drag, and eat regular, so I done my best to get educated. Just when I am beginning to kid myself that my line is about complete, this winter sports thing bust right over my head.

In the good old days, when the last hunting party was in, and the cayuses run out to winter range in the foot hills, we could put in the next six months spending our summer stake, and lying to each other about the game we got, and the funny things our pilgrims said and did. There was a big old stove in the bar at the King Edward Hotel, and the bad horses that was rode, and the fighting grizzlies shot around it during the winter, was nobody's business.

Then we got all spraddled out on winter sports. Some misguided yahoo got to ghost dancing, and figures that here's the place will make San Moritz look like a dirty deuce. "We got snow, and scenery, hills for skis and toboggans. Let's put this man's town on the map as the winter playground of America."

And the hell of it is, we fall for it. Even Ike Mills himself sent up to Le Pas, and imported a flock of Huskies, and goes in for "mushing." He kept the team in an old barn back of the Methodist Church and when the faithful got to praising the Lord in song, them halfbred wolves all pointed their noses to the moon and joined in. There ain't any winter sports where the Rev. Hackleberry says we are headed for.

Then we all mucked in, and cleared the snow off the Bow river, and the fancy skating class holds forth there. Fancy is the right word, too. Kate Clark—who's a living ad for the boarding house she runs and don't weigh an ounce over 210—doing her outside edges, also her left ears, is a marvel of grace and agility. It's a right good thing she is overstuffed, and sort of bounces, or that rink would have been a dead loss pronto.

Meanwhile a bunch of energetic hombres have cleared the stumps and brush off Caribou Hill, and built a toboggan slide. The first quarter mile ain't quite straight up and down, then it flattens out enough so you can get a couple lungfuls before it drops right out from under you. Jim Stink, our w.k. laundry expert, sizes it up and says, "Whaffor lie on belly—WHEE-E-E. Walka milee back. Clazy." He ain't so far wrong that.

However, me and Buckshot figure you don't have to be strong or graceful to do it, so we take a fall out of it. The first time ain't so worse, so we decided another whirl won't do any harm. We are doing about ninety miles an hour when I open my eyes just long enough to see Bill Davey's pig ambling across the track. When I open 'em again, Doc Robinson is telling the crowd to stand back and give me air. Buckshot is some used up too, so for a while we just give the sports our moral support.

If we had knew enough to keep on with moral support we would have saved ourselves a heap of grief, but that's the trouble with us Canucks— never know when we are beat, till somebody pounds it in with a neck yoke.

Cliff White has been East, and got hipped on skiing, and throws a mean line of talk. First thing, he educates us to calling it skeeing and not skying. Then he has me all popped up, so I see myself gliding graceful as a eagle soaring, guiding flocks of pilgrims all winter, at so much a guide, who have all quit Switzerland, Lake Placid, and such two-bit dumps, for the winter playground of America.

I send for a book all about it, and when it comes it's the one that was translated into the Scandinavian. Lars Larsen is cutting cordwood way the other side of Squaw Mountain, so I snowshoe out, and have to promise the old thug a bottle of gin and $4 to call it a day, and come to town. When we get there, and I confront him with the book, I find out that he played in hard luck in his youth, and can't read. He holds me to the gin and dollars though. I try to collect part of it from the publicity fund of the Canadian Rocky Mountain Winter Sports Association, they take the quibbling stand that I should have found out before I lugged Lars in to town. However, there's plenty of pictures in the book so we study them.

Half a dozen optimists sent East for skis, etc., and, ten days after, the whole village turns out to see us ride 'em. Buckshot tried to cinch his onto high-heeled riding boots, and it just naturally won't work. Me, I try moccasins, and, while it's better than Buck's rig, most of the time I have one on and the other coming or going.

For the next few days the sucking ski runners sneak off into the bush and practice "in camera" as the police court reports say.

I want to give it a miss, but Cliff sings his siren song, about the demand there will be for skiing guides, and I stay with it. It's a great day in my life when I go down to the post office, stepping like I was travelling on eggs, and with a death grip on those poles with little wheels on em, and turn round without going all round the block.

On my way back to the shack, I meet a Mountie who has been bitten by the bug, too, and he says, "What's the matter with us taking some grub, and skiing out to that dump of yours at Spray Lakes? A little cross-country practice is all we need, before we start learning Telemarks and Christianias." "Listen, Bull," I horned in, "if ever I get as far as Spray and back on these thus and so Scandahoovian slipping planks, I shall be plumb satisfied to rest on my well-earned laurels the rest of the winter. Telegrafs and Christine can wait for all of me." Everyone in these hills knows I'm easy, though, and I fall for another session of education.

It's thirty miles from town to my place at Spray, and we decide not to rush, but to take two days each way, maybe laying over a day at the Lakes. The Bull gets him a week's leave, and early Saturday morning the band of Christian maryrtrs meet at my shack. Each of us has a bed roll and a week's grub hunt on him. I feel like the youth in Excelsior we learned about in grade four, only I would a damn sight sooner have packed a banner than fifty pounds not counting an ax and frying pan I have got.

THINGS DIDN'T GO TOO AWFUL bad until we hit the first hill. It's steep and the trail makes a bend at the bottom. The Bull takes off first, and makes it pretty good. Buckshot follows, but his pack gets going faster than he is, so he sits down, by way of putting on the brakes. I shove off, and pass Buck like a bat out of hell, but can't make that turn. I try stem turns, jump turns, telemarks, and a lot that ain't in our book, and finish in a nose dive, with kind of a tail spin, and come to a perfect fourteen-point landing, losing hide on all fourteen of 'em, believe it or not.

From then until dusk it's one long-drawn out session of struggle up one side, slide down the other, and crash at the bottom. Did you ever try to get up out of about four feet of snow, with fifty pounds on your back, an ax handle in your ribs, and a frying pan round your neck?

After a while we don't even cuss. We've used 'em all up. I know damn well we could have averaged better time travelling on snowshoes backwards, but we came to ski and, by the shriveled-up hindquarters of Astor's pet goat, we are going to ski. We camped that night under a big old spruce, all of ten miles from town.

After we got a big fire going and a quart or so of tea into us, we climbed into our snoozing sacks and tried to sleep. I feel like I'd been running through a threshing machine, and can't say I got much sleep that night. Judging from the groans and language seeping through the winter night, I ain't the only one.

About three A.M. we are froze out, so stiff it takes all that dogged determination the sharps tell us made Canada a great Nation, to bend down and hitch on the Norwegian man killers. Every last one of us would have liked to head home, but we think of the horse laugh, and decide to die for dear old Whatsit.

The Bull has blisters the size of four-bit pieces on both feet. Every time Buckshot moves he creaks, and me, the seat of my pants is just four inches from the ground. It begins to thaw, and the snow gets sticky. Pretty soon we are not only shoving those sleigh runners, but about half a ton of gooey snow with 'em. We haven't learned about wax, so we plug along. Then I decide a live coward has it all over a dead hero like a tent, and I take the blame things off, tie 'em together, set the pack in the middle, and by hooking the poles through the harness, make a sort of sleigh of the works. By keeping in our tracks, I can just about navigate.

When we do get back to town we'll tell the rest of the winter sports what a whale of a time we had, and make big medicine about where the next trip will be.

What I want to know is, what the next complication will be. Nobody's going to kid me into hunting sheep from an airplane.

The Sportsman, January 1931, 44–45

SIX

Rams

This is one of the "straight pieces." The language is terse and under control, though a few westernisms creep in: cayuses, for example, and the pragmatic saying, ascribed to "The Indians here, who are mighty hunters," "Any gun good, shootem good." The topic, theme and tone are close to his stories written in character as Tex, but the language is correct and fluid— almost bland by comparison. Tex's gifts of characterization and description come through here, even if there is no scope for his usual irony and gentle mockery. Details concerning the work of an outfitter/guide, such as the stacking of camp materials to hand in case of snow, to facilitate set-up, add a sense of reality and nearness to the material. The details of the hunt itself might interest hunters, given the enormous changes in animal stock, techniques and legal regulations since that time. Here Tex also mentions the ram he shot for the collection of the Smithsonian, meant to represent a normal animal, not a trophy head; this is one of a very few mentions of his long-term relationship with the Smithsonian.

—AG

Rams

———— • ————

There is no hunting like the hunting of the Ovis canadensis
By N. Vernon-Wood

THE SCIENTIFIC NAME is *Ovis canadensis,* but to the hunters and guides of the Canadian Northwest, they are just "rams."

North of the main line of the Canadian Pacific Railway, on the eastern slopes of the Rockies, this king of the high places reaches perfection. A national park, embracing some four thousand square miles of natural breeding grounds and pastures in which all animal life is rigidly protected, extends from the foothills to the Great Divide, and all native big game, especially big-horn, have increased to an almost incredible extent during twenty years of strict conservation. The natural overflow maintains a constant supply of trophies for the hunter in the territory adjacent to the park.

The village of Banff, in Alberta, is the only settlement of any size within the park, and from here the pack trains strike off each season into the ram country. An outfit leaving the village is one of the most picturesque sights of the modern West. Following the guide in single file comes a string of cayuses—blacks, bays, buckskins, and pintos—shaggy, homely as sin, but sure-footed, hardy, and wise; each loaded with around one hundred and fifty pounds of grub, dunnage, and camp paraphernalia. The pilgrim with the cook and wrangler follow. All visitors are divided into three parts like ancient Gaul: "tourists," "tin canners," and "pilgrims." Any old visitor is a tourist provided he or she comes by train. The tin canners explain themselves, but as soon as one mounts a cayuse and takes to the hills with an outfit, to hunt, fish, climb, or just loaf, then he or she becomes a pilgrim, and as such is accepted into the inner circle.

Three or four days' travel through a land of peaks, glaciers, gemlike lakes, and tumbling streams brings the outfit to the ram country. Alpine meadows well above timber line—which is here at an altitude of 7,500 feet —broken by almost inaccessible ledges are the favored haunt of the big fellows. Here on wind-swept slides and grassy benches, sheep, stag, elk, and moose hold forth until the snows of late fall drive the antlered beasts down to the shelter of the forest, but the rams remain, high on the ridges, where snow does not accumulate to any great extent.

Most guides have their favorite places in which to establish the hunting camp. Pasturage for the pack string, wood and water and proximity to timber line are the prime requisites. Often the same spot is used year after year. When you arrive at such a camp the tent and tepee poles will be found carefully stacked against a large tree, so that they will be in plain sight in the event of arriving during or after a snowstorm, and there will be wood, piled under the overhanging branches of a spruce, that a fire may be started quickly.

CAMP MAKING, where every man has his job and does it, takes a surprisingly short time. The cook tent, in which the collapsible stove is erected, is the first consideration. While other tents or tepees are being pitched, the wrangler strips the ponies of saddles and blankets and piles all equipment in an orderly heap which is covered by the canvas pack mantles, as a protection against both weather and the nocturnal porcupine. What a porky can do to an unprotected saddle in the course of a night is a crime. Meanwhile, the cook has been doing his stuff, and before you realize it a meal is prepared. "Come an' get it or I'll chuck it to the mooses," is an invitation to drop everything and gather round.

One's first glimpse of *O. canadensis*, grace and poise in every line of him, head held regally, standing nonchalantly on the edge of a sheer chasm, is a sight for the gods. I have hunted him over a period of twenty years, and still nothing can thrill me as the sight of sheep. Rams, while stationary, are not easy to distinguish, so beautifully do they blend with the limestone cliffs and the autumnal color of the vegetation. Only when on snow fields, or silhouetted on the sky line, do they show plainly, and the novice will require quite a bit of practice to spot them easily.

A mature animal weighs from 325 to 350 pounds, and stands around forty inches at the shoulder. Looking over some notes, I find that the ram which I killed for the Smithsonian Institute, to be placed in a group as representative of an average sheep, had an overall length of sixty inches. The curl of the horn measured thirty-six inches. It was not a large head, but just what he was to represent, an average ram.

The largest head on record, as far as I know, was killed in the Banff district, and he had a curl of forty-nine and three quarter inches on the right horn, and forty-eight on the left. The runner-up also came from north of Banff, and goes forty-seven and five eights and forty-five and a half respectively. Truly noble trophies.

The freshly-skinned head, with cape attached, will weigh fifty pounds, quite enough to back-pack down a mountain, after a strenuous day's stalking.

When the points of the horns do not reach the level of the eyes, don't shoot, but look for another and worthier trophy. When, however, the "curl" has reached the eye, the head begins to be worth while, and this is the basis used by most guides in sizing up a prospective shot.

Almost without exception, the tips of the horns on mature rams are rubbed and broken, frequently four or more inches being missing. The popular explanation for this is that the points are broken during the annual fighting of the rutting season. Personally, I do not agree with this. When fighting, the impact is taken on the curl just above the base, and in that position it is impossible for the tips to come together. Moreover, I do not think that even two grown rams, fighting as enthusiastically as they do, could come together with enough force to break the horns. The more reasonable explanation is that sheep themselves rub the points, because of interference with the vision. I have watched them working on the rocks rubbing and prying in an endeavor to shorten the points to a place below the eyes. Occasionally one finds a head with a sweeping curl, bringing the horns well forward of the line of vision. Here there has been no incentive to rub, and a perfect head is the result.

The flesh of mountain sheep is delicious; most mountain men agree that it is the finest of any game meat. The skin is practically useless; the hair, like that of the deer species, is hard and brittle. Don't ever make the mistake of having a skin tanned with the hair on, thinking it will make a rug for the den. In about two weeks you will find sheep hair in the morning coffee, and eventually you will have to sneak out some dark night and throw the thing over the bridge, if you value peace in the home.

For keenness of vision, scent, and hearing the ram stands unsurpassed;

the sight especially seems to be absolutely telescopic. The slightest movement, even at great distances, is instantly detected, so that, with the difficulties of the terrain added to the elusiveness of the game, a successful stalk is no mean achievement.

Rams have a weakness, however, which the experienced hunter will work to his advantage, where possible. With the exception of the eagle, which takes his toll of young lambs, all enemies of the mountain sheep come from below. *Ergo*, if humanly possible approach him from above, even if this means a circuit of several miles. In his pride as monarch of the crags, he seems to think that as long as he keeps the lower slopes under observation he is invulnerable. When alarmed he will almost invariably climb, another trait that the hunter can often work to his advantage. I remember, while hunting with Colonel Weems, topping out on a long ridge. Below us, but out of range for anything but a very lucky shot, were six or seven rams, feeding quietly. It was impossible to descend the other slope, because of the general steepness and lack of cover. I told the colonel that I would fire a shot or two in the general direction of the bunch, and that in all probability they would climb. It didn't make much of a hit with him, but as it was his only chance of getting a shot at that bunch he agreed to try anything once. I moved a few hundred yards along the crest of the ridge, and opened fire. At the first report, the rams bunched up, apparently at a loss as to what to do about it. The second report started them, and by the good luck that sometimes does attend a guide, they climbed straight for the colonel. He killed his ram, at about fifty yards.

Stalking rams, however, is not a simple matter of getting above a bunch, selecting your trophy, and returning to camp in triumph. An ever-present source of grief is the wind. While in the valley it may be blowing steadily from the west, as soon as one reaches the higher slopes and ridges it comes from every point. It swirls and eddies like the rapids of streams. A sudden change in temperature causes a down draft, and a cliff turns it from west to east. Your ram, a mile away and out of sight, catches a whiff of man and goes from here to there with celerity, often putting two ranges between himself and the ledge where you last saw him, and after stalking carefully you find nothing.

Again, a position may be attained well above, but too far away for a reasonable shot. Cover is scarce, and after what seems hours of lying in wait, hoping he will feed upwards, a marmot spies you, and immediately, with that piercing whistle of his, alarms every living beast within sound. Or, just as you think everything is going to work perfectly, a young ram with a twenty-inch head, who has been feeding hidden by a fold on the hillside, walks into view. He dashes away with a clatter of loose shale, and your quarry immediately does likewise, not standing on the order of his going.

All this adds to the delight of the hunt, and when success crowns one's efforts the knowledge that no easy trophy has been secured adds much to one's satisfaction.

WHEN LEAVING CAMP to stalk rams, take no unessentials along. Rifle, ammunition, and the clothing worn will be enough to carry over slide, shale, cliff, and rock face.

It is not my intention to suggest the type of rifle. Every man to his taste. The Indians here, who are mighty hunters, have this saying, "Any gun good, shootem good." Do not, though, do as so many hunters do—leave the sighting in of a new gun until you are in the game country, or, worse still, take it for granted that the sighting was done at the maker's.

In the matter of clothing, use woolen underwear, so that the body sweat will be absorbed without leaving a clammy and cold rag next your skin. Wear good climbing boots, well nailed, and two pairs of woolen socks to cushion the feet against rocks. Take an extra sweater in the ruck sack, for lunch time and while your guide is skinning. The winds of autumn at this altitude are, to say the least, fresh, and after the climb you will undoubtedly be heated. A hat with wide brim is a protection from sun, and will also keep rain from trickling down the back of your neck. Khaki or dead grass colors, of course.

The end of the day will probably find you some miles from camp, dog tired and hungry. After what seems hours of slogging through fallen timber, muskeg, or what not, at last the flicker of a camp fire through the trees. Then the odor of coffee.

The evening meal over, after a pipe by the crackling camp fire and some talk of this and that, camp becomes silent. As you lie in your sleeping bag, listening to the faint tinkle of the horse bell, the distant hoot of an owl, and the ever-present music of running streams, whether or not the day has been crowned by success, you will decide, as so many good sportsmen have done, that there is no hunting like the hunting of rams.

The Sportsman, April 1931, 67–68

SEVEN

TEPEE TALES

The framing device in this story is rather different from the others. The author puts himself in the position of a client from New York, with his wife, who solicits hunting stories from "Jim and Buck," who are happy to oblige. The Buck character clearly stands in for Tex, with his experience of guiding a party from New York for over twenty years, as Tex did. Tex's virtuosity as a story-teller comes through here too, in his impersonation of a character significantly more grizzled and less tempted than he was to intersperse erudite Latinisms and Latin puns, Scriptural allusions or other language games into a "mountain man" narrative. The fact that he is able credibly to frame the story this way, himself playing the urbane narrator, suggests a good deal about the ambivalence of his actual position vis-à-vis his colleagues and his customers in the mountains.

—AG

Tepee Tales

———————•———————

"Any bird that tries to bluff you he ain't ever scared is a liar by the clock"
By N. Vernon-Wood

It had become an established custom, as soon as the evening dishes were washed and the kindling wood cut and covered for the morning's fires, for us to sit around in the guide's tepee, yarning and smoking. After the first few days on the trail, and we had, as Buck Foster, our guide, put it, "gotten the feel of each other," we looked forward to the evening call, "They's a fire in the tepee." Buck, Jim the wrangler, and Joe the cook never wearied of asking questions about New York and the manner of life there, while we, on the other hand, drew them to tell of experiences on the trails and trap lines, and the old ranching days of Alberta.

Jim had just told of an experience of the year previous, when a she-grizzly with two cubs had invaded his camp and gone thoroughly through the grub pile. Not having a rifle in camp, he had tried to drive them away by banging two frying pans together and yelling like an Indian. "She didn't bluff worth a dime, an' when she thought I was gettin' too close to her blame family she made a run at me. What did I do? Man, I lit out of that on the high lope, and left her to it. I bet I bust three or four world's records for the hundred, two hundred, and half-mile dash. Scared pink, I'll tell a man."

"I thought nothing ever frightened you men," my wife said.

"Don't you ever believe it, ma'am," Buck chimed in. "Any bird that tries to bluff you he ain't ever scared is worth watchin'. He's a liar by the clock.

"The year I went into this guidin' business, I got me a jolt that darn near made me quit before I got right started. Only thing that saved me was we were ten days' travel from the railway, and I had to stick, or walk back and lose my wages.

"I'd got the notion I was a bronco fighter, and was bustin' them for old Colonel Wyndham on the Anchor S outfit. One mornin', I climbed onto the middle of a big rangy sorrel, and after he had cat-hopped couple of times he rared up and sort of stood weavin' on his hind legs. Just as I loosened up in the saddle a mite, he threw himself backwards, an' me not being quick enough, he fell on top. When I come back to earth, I was on a mattress on the buckboard, bein' rushed to the Holy Cross Hospital in Calgary, and feelin' like someone had took out my innards and put 'em back all wrong.

"I got out of the hospital in August, and the doc told me I was through riding for keeps, and that I should go to Banff and sort of loaf. I came up to Banff all right, but the doc didn't know that a saddle, bed roll and seven dollars real money was all he had left me with to loaf on. It looked like a long slim winter for old man Foster's boy, but the first guy I run into in Banff was Watty Potts, that used to night hawk for the PX outfit south of the Hat.

"He was in this dude wranglin' game, and he told me the outfit he worked for could use a good horse jingler. 'All you got to do,' he told me, 'is herd in a few gentle old pack ponies to camp in the mornin', cut wood, and throw bull to pilgrims from New York, Boston, and such points. Biggest cinch in Alberta.'"

"Times have sure changed," said Jim. "All a wrangler does now is forty-seven separate and distinct jobs, and cut wood while he's restin'. If he gets a chance to wash the odd shirt once a month he's playing in luck."

"Yeah? Well, I tell you something else; I was a right good little jingler, an' we didn't lose any time getting from here to there because old Baldy wasn't in the herd this mornin', or take about an hour to catch a colt mornings. I got all of $35 a month, an' what we couldn't carry in our slickers we left behind. What I pay you Tim Eaton cowboys a month was a whole winter's stake them days, and you carry more dunnage than a horse can jump over. Times have changed all right." This from Buck, who like all old-timers was convinced that times were not what they were, and that men were like the times.

"Well, as I was sayin'," when this ex-shuffler interrupted, "we pulled out from town with two couples from the East. Our route lay over the Vermilion Pass to the Kootenay, over to the Columbia, and up Toby Creek through the

Selkirks to Lardeau on the East Kootenay Lake. One pair of pilgrims were going to take the steamboat there, and go back by the Crow's Nest Railway, and the others were coming back by trail to Banff. Everyday we was out, I could feel myself getting more like a white man, though I was still sort of spooky.

"As soon as we got into the Selkirks the country got different. The valleys are deep and narrow, horse feed is scarce, and the cedar forest is so darn thick that it's sort of dusk all the time. Goffy sort of layout, and not so pleasant as the Rockies—to my mind anyways.

"I began to have grief with the herd, trying to hit back for the Columbia and good feed. Most every night I had to roll out of the old saddle blankets, an' discourage 'em.

"There was a little old ornery pinto in the bunch that I knew more than most men, and she was always leadin' the rest of the knot-heads. I got so I strung lash ropes from the trees across the trail, and built more fences than would have done some farmers.

"We crossed Earl Grey's pass, and got down Hamil creek to within a day's ride of Lardeau, and the pilgrims decided that next morning the two for the boat would leave us, with Watty and a pack horse, while the rest of us had a field day in camp and washed the other pair of socks. Then at the last minute the other he-pilgrim decides he might as well go along, which left his wife and me to hold down the camp.

"I rustled the herd in right soon in the morning, an' they got away to a good start. Then I cut enough wood to do us the rest of the stay, and after splicing a busted last rope I caught up on a little sleep. That evening, Mrs. Van Deiman and I sat around the campfire until pretty late, talking of this an' that, every so often me dashing into the bush to head off those misguided hay burners.

"I don't know how long after we had turned in, I heard the bell on that pinto misfit coming down the trail, and I was peevish as hell when I rolled out again to head 'em off. I took a two-handed club along, figuring if I got close enough to bend it over her ribs. There wasn't any moon, an' that valley was dark as the insides of a black cat anyway, but about hundred yards from camp I saw something looming up that I thought was the white patches on the worthless hide of the pinto. I lets a whoop out of me and took a swipe at it. Whatever it was I missed it, an' it went 'spit-t-t,' and went up a tree scratchin' an' snarlin' like all get out. Do you expect me to look you between the eyes an' say I wasn't scared? It can't be done. Say, I was back into the camp an' into the blanket in three jumps, an' I swear I shoved down three four good-sized cedars getting there."

"Mrs. Van woke up and asked what was the matter. I told her I had taken a wallop at a cayuse, and it had gone up a tree. She came out of her tent with a little pearl-handled .38 revolver, and says, 'Take this and see what it was.'"

"'Woman,' I told her, 'that gun ain't one quarter big enough for me right now. What I need is a howitzer.' What was it? Cougar I guess, but I wasn't used to the hills them days, and I knew it was the Koosey Onck itself that night. For a week after, every time Watty got rid of his eatin' tobacco I jumped a foot."

Continued Buck, "At that, being scared on your own account ain't quite so bad as being all spooked up about the other guy."

"I guided a New York pilgrim on an' off for twenty years. Naturally, we got pretty close to each other in that time, an' I often wish they was a couple million more like him. A sportsman an' a gentleman that done you good just to know.

"Like the rest of us, he wasn't gettin' any younger, so the last few seasons all the huntin' we did hardly kept steak in the skillet, but he was plumb contented to be out where he could see the ice fields hangin' on the slopes of the Divide, cast the odd fly, an' smell balsam.

"Then one fall he brought out a nephew, fresh from college, and just rearin' to go. 'Work hell out of him Buck, an' don't let him think big-game hunting is too easy,' is the old chief's word to me, an' I sure done my best. When he wasn't going up we was sliding down, an' nine hours a day on a mountain sure was doing its stuff for the young feller's legs an' wind.

"Any of you birds ever took an outfit to the head of Glacier Lake? Well, there isn't much of a trail, an' about the best way is to hit the edge of the water after you get past the stream at the outlet. The lake is plenty deep and two jumps from the edge you're into twenty feet of cold glacier-fed drink.

"He had got about two thirds of the way down the lake when I hear a splash an' a holler from the pack string, an' looked back to see three of the knotheads swimming.

"There was a big old dry spruce had blown down, an' fell from the bank out into the lake. We had weasled our way round the up-ended roots, but these three know-it-all cayuses decided the easiest way was to take to the lake an' swim round the windfall.

"It wouldn't have been so bad, only old Tom got hung up by a loose bight of lash rope gettin' wound up in a snag that was sticken out of the trunk, an' while he was swimmin' like hell he wasn't gettin' any place. That sort of put it up to me, so I slipped my skinning knife into my teeth and jumped in. I had quite a job cutting the fool horse loose, but just about the time I thought I should freeze stiff an' drown with old Tom things came loose, an' I grabbed a handful of tail, an' we steamboated to shore together.

"While we were doing our Annette Kellerman act, the old chief had grabbed the most important pack horse in the outfit and had him stripped and the bottle out. The snifter he poured into me when I came ashore was one of those drinks that stick out in your mind like your first pair of spurs or your weddin' day, an' such events.

"As luck had it, we could make camp right there as there was a slide with horse feed on it, an' plenty dry wood. Some of our duffle needed a drying, and the sugar was a dead loss. Next morning I sent the wrangler back toward the Saskatchewan to put up a couple of bars on the trail in case the ponies took a notion to back track, an' suggested that the young feller take his rifle an' go along to sneak up on the lick where the outlet from the lake hits the main river. You can often pick a goat up there, without busting yourself climbing a million feet.

"Then the cook an' I started to do what we could to salvage the wet grub, an' dry out our whatnots.

"Just after lunch we heard a flock of shots coming from the mountain above us, an' I took the glasses to see if it was our outfit, or if somebody else was in the valley. I couldn't locate anything, though, and didn't think much about it for a while.

"Later on I wondered why the boys weren't back in camp by now, an' walked down the lake a bit to look around. Then way up on the rocks I spotted our two hunters, trying to work their way down. I got quite a jolt as I could see they couldn't ever make it an' they was dropping' right for the edge of a sheer rock wall.

"Nephew was wearin' a clean white sweat shirt, when he left camp that morning, an' I could see this white spot sort of eatin' along. Only once in a while I made out the wrangler. His clothes didn't show up so good.

"It didn't do any good to yell as they was too far up to tell what I said, so I just thought that when they found out it wasn't any use they would climb back an' come down the way they must have went up. Try an' imagine what I felt like when just then I saw the white shirt slip, slide a few feet, and then make a plunge, hit a little ledge an' bound out into nothing at all, then crash a hundred feet straight down. It struck a second, and then rolled slowly into a crevice out of sight. Man, oh man, you could have bought me for a lead dime.

"I high-tailed for camp, an' got a lariat, telling the biscuit builder to get another an' ooze out after me, not letting the old chief catch on. Then we tore up the slide like two cats that had been shot in the tail by boot-jacks. We figured we might, by the grace of God, get to where we could rope ourselves down to the crevice, and do what little seemed would want doin'. I knew that no man could make that fall and be worth anything to anybody except an undertaker. We went up places we would have been dizzy on, in cold blood. Finally, we had to hang up a minute to figure out just how to get from here to there, and suddenly remembered we had a wrangler somewhere on that mountain. I let a holler out of me, and he answered from above, and not so far way, although we couldn't see each other. Then imagine how bright old world looked when we heard our young pilgrim yell, 'Can we get down to you, Buck?'

"'Hell's bells, no. Get to blazes back up an' come down the long hog-back on the east end. An' what the thus an' so you two damn fools think you doing anyway?' There ain't enough words in or out of old Webster's masterpiece to do justice to just how I felt. Also by the time old greasy an' I have got back to where we don't have to hang on by our finger nails and eyebrows, we have invented quite some new ones. Long after dark our heroes drag their tails into camp, an' we get the details.

"Just after they left camp the spotted a herd up to hell an' gone on the cliffs, an' decided to bust them one. After a lot of hard going, they plaster a billy, but he slips over a couple of ledges, an' it takes them quite some to time to locate him. Not being very expert at skinning they decide to take plenty of hide with the head, and let me finish the job when they got to camp. Nephew makes a pack of it and the shirt, fastens his cartridge belt around it, and they decide they can get down without going way round the easy route. The going of course gets worse and no better, and at last they have to hand the hide and rifle to each other as one passes the other and gets set. What I saw was the wrangler handing it down to our pilgrim and both of 'em sort of fumbling the job, so away it went and what I thought was nephew in the sweat shirt was the hide of that defunct billy.

"I cussed the pair of 'em out plenty an' I guess that shirt, belt, and hide are still in the crevice, an' if anybody wants it they can go get it. I ain't lost anything around there, me."

Joe grinned, and turning to Buck said, "Remember how the price of fur went up in '17? Well, I was sort of foot-loose that fall. The Army wouldn't take me, on account of them toes I froze off coming in from the Red Deer the winter before, so I figured I might as well run me a trap line. I went onto the Simpson and fixed up that old cabin at the forks, and run out a few loads of grub and traps before the snow flew. By the time I had got organized, and a pile of word cut, and the line run, winter was on us with a whoop and holler. Things went good right from the start.

"One morning I found a pippin of a steel-blue lynx in the first set, and not wishing to spoil his hide by shooting him with the .45, I took off a snowshoe and rapped him over the nose with it. He sort of kicked over and I took his foot out of the trap, and went to resetting it. A lynx is funny about traps. Get him by two toes, and he plants right there. A coyote or wolverine would tear things all to hell and get out, but the cats quit cold. Anyway, while I am working on the trap, I see out of the corner of my eye puss get up and stagger for the timber. That was $50 getting out of there, so I make a flying leap and grab him by the scuff of the neck and reach for my gun and beat him over the head with it. He dies again, and I finish the trap, pick him up by a front and hind leg, and sling him over my shoulders, figuring to take him to the shack and skin where it's warm.

"I've just got in sight of the cabin when that bobtailed hellion come to life again, and let out a snarl right in my ear, and reached round with his free front paw and ripped my Mackinaw right up the front. That's another time when I ain't scared, if you don't care what you say. I heaved that lynx forty feet up in the air and then piled on him again. This time, though, I sat in the middle of him till I got my gun unlimbered and shot him at a range of about two inches. You would have thought it was a moose yard where we fought the last battle—ten acres of snow tramped and rolled plumb flat. It's like Buck says, a man can get plenty scared."

To which Buck added, "I'm scared right now, that if you guys don't get off my bed an' let me grab a little sleep we won't get breakfast before we break camp tomorrow."

The Sportsman, September 1931, 52–54 and 58

EIGHT

An Early Ski Attempt on Mt. Ptarmigan

This article about the first ski attempt in the Canadian Rockies was written for *The Canadian Alpine Journal,* the official journal of the Alpine Club of Canada (ACC) since 1907. For many years, *The Canadian Alpine Journal* was the principal place where important landmarks in mountaineering in Canada or by Canadians who were members of the ACC were described and recorded. The purpose of these articles was to provide documentation about new routes, as well as provide evidence (sometimes contested by other Club members) of important and difficult ascents. At this time, the ACC was a scientific organization as well as a serious mountaineering club, and so Tex did not write this article in his Tex persona, but as the educated (even slightly Romantic) Nello Vernon-Wood who rhapsodizes about the beauty of the peaks even as he tells us their precise heights. It is worth contrasting this story with "Us Winter Sports," where Tex pokes fun at his poor skiing (presumably he was a better skier than this if he was in the climbing party) and is suspicious about the building of a ski lodge. There is no evidence of that comedy here about similar events, and so this article demonstrates how completely Tex/Nello could adopt a convincing writing persona and see the world through those eyes.

—JR

An Early Ski Attempt
on Mt. Ptarmigan

———————— • ————————

By N. Vernon-Wood

In addition to any other function it may have in the scheme of things, a mountain is a challenge. It arouses one's curiosity. Can it be climbed, what will one see behind and beyond? To the outdoorsman, it seems to say, "Come, test your legs and heart and courage." Many men and women have accepted the gauge of the peaks since first De Saussure and Pacidus a Spescha braved the terrors and difficulties of the unknown in Europe. Virgin peaks decrease in number ·with each year, but be the ascent the first or the fifty-first the satisfaction of proving oneself and theories, of overcoming the physical difficulties incident to any major climb is rich reward. A day spent in intimate contact with almost overwhelming grandeur is reward pressed down and running over.

During the winter of 1930 a small group of ski enthusiasts were prospecting the hills and alplands in the vicinity of Banff for a suitable location in which to establish a permanent camp for the use of an ever increasing number of fellow skiers and mountaineers.[1] Most of the winter was passed travelling with back-packs over the passes and through the valleys seeking an ideal combination of snow conditions, slopes free from avalanche hazard, reasonable accessibility, and scenic excellence. In Skoki valley,[1] immediately north of Lake Louise, they found their desideratum.

1. On the Skoki valley, with a mention of this ascent, see Passes of the Canadian Rockies on David Birrell's PeakFinder: http://www.rmbooks.com/Peakfinder/

Here, conditions, approximated the best of European ski centres, slopes on which the novice may try his 'prentice hand, open alplands, spruce filled valleys. The expert has an almost unlimited choice of slopes and hazards where great speeds and lightning turns may be executed. The valley is dominated by the Ptarmigan massif. Ptarmigan peak rises 10,070 feet, Richardson 10,125, and Pika, 10,015. The northern slopes are glacier hung, with a stupendous ice-fall terminating in a small unnamed lake of surprising beauty.

While engaged in building the log cabins which constitute the camp, the group often paused to gaze at the tempting slopes, and discuss the feasibility of a ski ascent of Ptarmigan. Possible routes were surveyed with the aid of field glasses, and it became a tacit understanding that soon the attempt would simply have to be made.

Spring had come to the lower valleys before the multitudinous duties of camp building were disposed of. Conversely, snow conditions at the higher altitudes had improved. A cornice that overhung a possible route fell under the accumulated weight of spring snow. The increasing power of the sun, thawing a little by day, made a crust which vastly improved ski travel, and at last on May 15th (1931) the party left the cabin to attempt the first ski ascent yet attempted[2] in the Canadian Rockies.

The altitude of camp is around 7000 feet, and from it the valley floor ascends gradually to the foot of a cliff, on top of which lies the nameless lake. The going was easy and, the lake crossed, a pause was made to come to a final decision as to route. The easier slopes swing westerly from the apex of the fan of the lower glacier. On examination this proved to be in danger of avalanche. The more difficult climb, under the cliffs that break the centre of the icefield, proved the safer. In an ever shortening series of traverses the point was reached, and the only really dangerous part of the ascent began. The rope adjusted, proceeding singly, each member of the party negotiated a sheer slope in a series of side steps to a narrow ledge, just wide enough for skis, leading to the ice-fall of the middle arm of the glacier. Later in the year this fall is badly crevassed, but at this time, an accumulation of snow from the upper icefields had filled or bridged

passes.asp?passname=Deception+Pass (accessed 9 February, 2007).

2. Original note: "The idea that this was the first ski ascent attempted has gained wide currency. Niall Rankin, in his article "Ski-ing in the Canadian Rockies" in the British Ski Year Book, 1932, repeats this error. For some prior ski climbs see the C.A.J. Vols. xix and xx. (Editor)."

them. The slope is very steep; a misstep meant an accident if not a tragedy. Fortunately a few inches of new powdery snow overlay the hard surface providing ideal footing for skis. At the end of each traverse ski poles had to be driven reversed into the snow to provide a safe anchorage while turning by means of the "kick."

By noon, the col between Ptarmigan and Pika had been reached and a pause for lunch on an exposed scree slope was welcomed. To the left the undulating stream of the upper glacier swept on to the summit. No crevasses appeared, and with the exception of a broken ridge about half way no great difficulty appeared. Rested and refreshed, skis adjusted, the final series of long swings commenced. As the peak came into full view, the disappointing fact was revealed, that the final 75 feet were bare of snow, and a complete ski ascent impossible. At three-thirty the snow limit was reached, and nothing further would be accomplished[3] by scrambling over the rocks. The aneroid registered exactly 10,000 feet, and in a cyclorama of titanic magnitude, a halt was called.

To the north was the Lake Louise group, Temple, Ten Peaks, Lefroy and Victoria, glacier hung and majestic. The valley of the Bow was immediately below with its waters visible here and there, flowing easterly, to drain at last in Hudson [sic] Bay. A little to the west the Kicking Horse, breaking through the famous pass of that name, hurried to the pacific. Southward the Douglases guarded the portals of the Red Deer valley. The world seemed snow-covered and silent. A brooding calm, accentuated occasionally by the roar of a distant avalanche.

The sun was sinking rapidly westward, and at 10,000 feet, even in May, freezing begins almost the instant the shadows appear. The return trail would be icy unless an immediate start was made, so with a last eyefilling glance the "ride" down began. And what a ride! The horizontal mileage to the lake at the foot is approximately one and a half miles. The vertical descent is 3000 feet. Twenty-five minutes later the party shot out onto the level surface, blood racing, nerves tingling, and spirits high with the satisfaction of a thing well tried.

In March of last year, A.N.T. Rankin of London, England, with his wife, the Lady Jean, accompanied by two of the original climbers made a ski ascent of Ptarmigan. This was one of a number of major ascents accomplished last spring.

3. Original [sour] note: "Except, perhaps, the ascent of the mountain. (Editor)."

In March, Messrs. White, Bennett, and Weiss conquered the Snow Dome, 11,340 and in May a Winnipeg party made a number of climbs. Doubtless these climbs are the fore-runners of a number of winter ascents. They proved the undoubted superiority of "downhill" ski technique as developed in the Arlberg.[4] The ability to negotiate steep slopes at high speed, turn quickly, and stop instantly are requisites for the ski-mountaineer.

However, the particular technique one favors is secondary to the game. There is a feeling of adventure in making a winter expedition into the heart of the high places, that one does not get at any other time. The beauty of the country, silent and glittering, is beyond description. The feeling of physical fitness worth the effort.

Canadian Alpine Journal, vol. 21 (1932), 135–137

---

4. Original note: "Hardly, as the majority of ski ascents up to the time of writing have been made by skiers who have not yet had the pleasure of seeing the Arlberg technique. (Editor)."

NINE

PIPESTONE LETTERS NO. 1

This is the first of a series of "Pipestone Letters" running through May of 1937. The Pipestone Creek comes down from Pipestone Canyon high in the Rockies, and is now in Banff National Park. In Tex's day, it was outside Park boundaries and one of his primary hunting grounds, where he had a cabin. The main fun in this piece is directed against a prospective customer, McPhee, who wastes Tex's time and his own with frivolous correspondence. But as in "William, Prepare my Barth," expectations of correct masculine behaviour while in the mountains shape the tone and content of the rest of this piece. The client arrives in "what the well-dressed club man is wearing" (by "club man," he meant the aristocratic and wanna-be aristocratic drones who frequented—and in a few places, still do frequent—gentleman's clubs). He needs some rough handling to make him shape up to expectations. Tex has to taunt him when he flags as they approach some game. Tex's slender physique has already been mentioned, even questioned, by the client, and now, in response to Tex's gender-loaded question why he didn't just come in summertime instead, to "pick posies and hunt butterflies," the client responds to both Tex's less-than-perfectly-masculine body and to his gendered insult: "By the red eyed old Jeehosophat, you slabsided long drink of pump water, if you can make it, I can." The client ends up "the dirtiest man between the Crow's Nest [Pass] and the Saskatchewan [River]." This dirt and his success in hunting signal his successful attainment of "mountain masculinity."

—AG

Pipestone Letters No. 1

———————•———————

By N. Vernon-Wood

—WB Ranch, Pipestone Creek
Alberta, Canada

To Mr. John Lincoln
Wall Street, N.Y.

Dear Friend,

When you made me promise to send you a letter every month, you shure cooked up a bunch of grief for me, but maybe in about ten years, I'll Get so I dont mind it, and be a second Mc. Pheel.

Mac wrote to me a few years back from the Knickerbocker Club, and said he wanted to hire six guides & seventeen ponies to bust out into the hills with. Could I supply same, & for how much? I told him Yes, & made a price. Then the rukus started. He sent another letter from the University club and said he wanted guides that were congenial & capable, and could haze a string without resorting to blasphemy, cussing, or plain bad language. That just about disqualified any jinglers I'd ever crossed trails with, but I needed the trip, and figured maybe the boys could coax a mile an hour out of the buzzard heads, without turning the wolves of orotory plumb loose, so I promised a flock of silver tongued wranglers.

The answer came from the Union League, and he said he expected the roughnecks to camp at least 100 yards from the Pilgrims. Thats all right by me, it will give the help a chance to catch up on the words they missed durin the day. It would take Doc Elliots five foot shelf to hold all the letters that bird sent, an in the end, he took a motor trip through the Rockies, in a car that had everything on it but the kitchen sink.

I asked another New Yorker, who come up that year, if he knew Mc. Pheel, "Shure," he says, "He made a wad of money & retired a year or so back. He hasnt many friends, or much to occupy his time, so he writes himself a letter from the Lotus Club, and addresses it to the Ritz. Then he hightails to the Ritz, and asks for his mail, gallops over to the Yale Club and answeres it." By the hand carved horns of Astors pet goat, I bet thats true, an Mac had picked on me to sort of fill out spare time with.

I get a bang out of tryin to figure what kind of camp mate a guy will make, from the letters he writes, and I bet all you Dudes do the same, when you read the line we peddle tryin to coax you out here to show you last years Elk tracks. An lots of times we both get fooled.

Seems to me, most city guys picture a guide as either a bow legged ex cow poke, full of hard likker an cuss words, or else a lumber jack, three axe handles an a plug of spittin tobacco between the eyes, an we generally expect a Pilgrim to be washin, Shaving, and cleaning his nails, when he ought to be scrambling up a slide to try and bust a bear.

I BOOKED A SHEEP HUNT one time, with a feller that said he had done considerable huntin in Maine, New Brunswick and such, and he didn't want any frills. Just the sort of outfit I would take, if I was going on my own. Me, when I go out I figure to travel comfortable. The days when a hunk of sow belly, a sack of flour, an a rifle an fish hook, was considered an outfit, have passed out for me. An extra horse load of fixins make an auful difference when it rains three four days at a time, or when the game aint rallying round like you hoped. A comfortable camp has saved many an outfit from developin into a sore head convention.

When my Pilgrim unloaded off the Trans Canada, he looked like "what the well dressed club man is wearin." I parked him in my shack to change his dry goods, an went down to the corral to tack a pair of front shoes on old Baldy, as I figured I'd shure need him to carry the extra wardrobe an toilet assesories.

Meantime, the hunter says to my wife, "Can your husband really climb, he appears awfully slim?" Well, says my home foreman, "I admit he has to stand twice in one place to cast a shadow, but he ought to be able to climb, he's all the time goin straight up."

Two three days later we made camp in the sheep country, in one of them September storms that make you wonder what all you did with your summers earnings. After it cleared, it was cold, an a wind blowing that was mighty thin. We oozed over a couple of ridges without seeing a thing, and quite late we spotted a small bunch of rams, in a pocket right under a glacier.

It took us quite a while to get around to that cirque, and the Pilgrims legs were getting sort of secondhand, but we didn't have much daylight left, so I kept plugging. I sort of forgot him as I got hopped up creeping on the bunch, which were just around the next shoulder of rock, an when I stopped to give him a chance to get organized, he wasn't there.

I backtracked, and found him squatting in the lee of a boulder, trying to get his fingures warm, an feeling fed up, tired, an to hell with it anyway. I tell him the bunch are only a few hundred yards ahead, but don't get any enthusiastic reaction.

WHEN A MAN gets low in his mind thataway, get him hostile, so I curl my lip at him an say, "So you're the bird thats so hard eh. Whyinhell didnnt you come out here in the summer so you could pick posies, an hunt butterflies? an a heap more to that effect. Pretty soon he damns me all over the place, an says, "By the red eyed old Jeehosophat, you slabsided long drink of pump water, if you can make it, I can." An in twenty minutes or so, he'd accumulated a head I was proud of myself.

After that, we got right friendly, an inside a week he was the dirtiest man between the Crows Nest & the Saskatchewan. He was too busy havin a good time to bother with what he called non-essentials. They was enough sheep gravey in his whiskers to do a roundup crew.

Which proves Solomon was dead right, when he said you cant look at a cayuse, an tell how high he'll buck.

Me an Jim are figuring on going onto the Simpson Summit pretty soon. We need a new rug for the shack, and theres the old grizzly ramming around up there.

So long, an Yours truly,
"TEX."

Hunting and Fishing, September 1932, 16

105

TEN

AN' ALL WE DO IS HUNT

Tex here begins with a theme that also appears in "Tex Reads his Permit," namely the idea that guides are nothing but poachers who have gone legal—this was an issue which was close to the bone for Tex, and the Warden in question certainly knew that. The jibe sounds right for the macho culture of western Canada in general and mountain men in particular, then or now. A similar sense of what is work and what is not still leads to a certain amount of mockery directed at people who work indoors, who "lay around close to the stove all winter, and [buy] their meat." The story is largely about the frustrations of guiding inexperienced "pilgrims" (big game hunters) in the mountains.

—AG

An' All We Do Is Hunt

By N. Vernon-Wood

ITS FUNNY HOW THE OTHER fellows job always looks better than the one you've got yourself, if any.

The other day a Game Warden blew into my place, on winter patrols, which he claimed was plumb unnecessary, all the poachers havin gone into the Guide business, an makin so much money they lay around close to the stove all winter, and bought their meat.

"You birds shure got a cinch," he says, "Always got company, a cook to build your bannok, pack horses to carry fancy doo funnies, an them Pilgrims give you real money for doin just what you'd do anyhow. Look at us, alone three quarters over half the time, got to keep the trails in shape for you an your dudes to ride over, an if one of 'em chucks his snipe into a mess of dry pine needles, we have to fight the fire. The Government allows us one old plug pack horse, an we travel poor as Indians, all for a hundred a month an furnish your own grub."

I didn't put up any argument, whats the use, but I thought a whole lot. I bet if that Warden had to nurse along a flock of Pilgrims for a month, He'd be crazy as Joe Smith's dog, that froze his tail barkin at the moon.

Three four years back, I started out on a hunt with three birds who ran me bowlegged before we got through. One of them had been out with me before, and for a Pilgrim was bush wise. For a while everything was finer than frog hair, and I began to kid myself that here's one trip that wont put any more silver threads among the rust, but I didn't have my fingures crossed.

We hunted in two couples, the Pilgrim thats had experience takin one of the others, and me concentratin on the Captain, who hasnt yet bust anything. There was plenty of bear sign, but for a couple of days the bear saw us first, and one evening as we are sort of planning the next days grief, the old Pilgrim springs a suggestion that he an the other feller take a couple of days rations and drop down one of the valleys to see if they can wrangle them a Moose.

I cant say I am all hopped up with the idea, but after all, there don't seem to be any reason why, so I tell 'em forty eleven different things what not to do, and next morning they pack their Ruck sacks, and we wish them So long, an good luck.

The Skipper & I barge off to see if we can find a grizzly thats deaf, blind, an got a cold in his nose, so we can Indian up on him before he goes from here to there, but this country is healthy as hell for bear, so we came back to camp in the evening feeling sort of discouraged.

Up till then, the weather had been just what the doctor ordered, but that night the clouds got low, so that when we crawled out of our flea bags next morning, the visibility is what you might call poor. Not a peak in sight, and sort of crimpy round the edges. The Skipper feels a little stale, and don't seem to be in any mad rush to hit the high spots, so that we are late getting organized.

Long about two o'clock, we were sittin in the lee of a big boulder, feeding our faces, when the Skipper says, "Holy cat, Tex, I forgot to bring any extra ammunition, all I have is the five shells that are in my rifle."

"Which by the way things are pannin out, is five too many" I said, and it aint any more than said, when about 200 yards away a grizzly looms up.

"What'll I do?" whispers the Skipper, all steamed up.

"Bust him where he's biggest, an when you get him down, keep him there." I tell him.

The Skipper took a long careful sight an lets drive. Old Eph, lets a beller out of him, an swung round, bitin at his flank. It aint till the third shot he goes down, an even then he is making plenty fuss. "Take your time, now an anchor him right" I says, but the Captain is too excited to hear anything.

Then that old Horribilus gets up, and starts our way, an it looks to me like he's making forty miles an hour. And is he hostile? I tell a man.

I offer my gun to the Captain, and tell him to get going, and get going quick, or there will be two little strangers in Hell for supper, but he don't

110

even hear me, so I line up my sights where I think they will do the most good, thinking meantime, that I will get just one shot, before that fool bear is all over us like a tent, when down he goes. That rush was his last effort.

By the time I've got him skinned, we both decide that we need the two fingers of Hudsons Bay, that a kill calls for, so we hightail for camp, feeling plumb chesty, and man, the yarn we will tell the Old Pilgrim. It gets better an wilder every minute.

The Old Pilgrim however is not in camp, and in no time at all it got dark, and still he don't show up. By midnight, I am beginning to ghost dance, an see him & his partner all spraddled out under some cliff they have slipped off, or up in a tree with six or seven grizzly tearin up the scenery below.

We build a big fire, and fire a shot at intervals. Nothing happens. Every time a coyote howls, I dash out of the teepee an answer, thinkin it's them but morning comes, an they don't.

THE WRANGLER & I start a rescue expedition, with ropes an first aid kits an what all. We cant even find a track until we have travelled five or six miles, when we pick 'em up on an old pack trail. Where the side valley hits the main branch of the Palliser, old Joe Blaney has a trapping shack, and when we get there, he is busy putting up wood. I asked him did he see any loose pilgrims around, an he told me "Shure, they stayed here night before last, aint they in camp yet?" We told him the trouble, and it seems they started out yesterday morning to hunt a side draw, an figured to cross the head of it, and come out on the summit where camp was. The only thing wrong with that was a cliff about a million feet straight up, on the summit side, that no man in his senses would even want to throw a stone down, let alone climb.

"Bet you four bits they're back in camp, right now listnin to the skipper kill that bear agen, an knocking the bottom out of the crock of rum" says the wrangler. It's as dark as the inside of a black cat when we drag ourselves into camp, but the cook & the skipper are holding it down alone. We all get spooky that night, and in the morning don't need any Big Ben to rouse us out. The cook and wrangler hit one way, and the skipper & me take another, landing back at Joe's shack early in the afternoon. I figure Joe will join in the merryment, an help comb the country.

"Did you run 'em down?" says Joe. What I said, aint fit for nice people to hear. Then Joe told us that the missin brethren had dragged it into his camp again last night. "They got jack potted up that draw, but thought they could make the summit by swinging around to the west, an got into a mess of brule. By the time they backtracked themselves it was gettin dark, an they were closer here than there, so they bunked with me again."

Fine, but whereinhell are they now, I wonder. "All I know, I put 'em on the trail to the pass," said Joe, "an if they didn't get to camp, I guess they missed it someplace, an are on the way back to the railroad. If they keep goin, an don't bust a couple of legs, they'll make it in a week."

Which is plumb encouragin to me. We all start up the trail, and track the absent loved ones for about two hours, when all sign peters out again. I sent the cook back to camp with the skipper, telling the cook to hobble him if necessary. I aint taking chances on losing the only Pilgrim I have left. Buck & I quarter the country good and proper, but no luck.

We spent that night under a spruce, thinking up cuss words to spring on them explorers, when as an if we ever catch up on 'em. I begin to think our job will be to build a box, an ship 'em east in the baggage car.

We used all the next day circlin the country 'till we were dizzy, an long about dark, strike for camp, hungry, tired, an decidin to quit guidin, an study for the ministry, or somthin soothin to the nerves.

About a mile from camp, we hear voices in the dark, an by the shrivelled up hind quarters of Abrahams pet goat, here are the lost battalion, with Joe hazin them along. I'm so tickled to see them, I don't even cuss. Seems they landed at their pet road house again last night, after trying to walk down an old moose they started up on their way up the trail yesterday. The moose circled, and as per usual, night found 'em a mile or so from Joes. I told Joe to send me his bill for board an room, and chewed the mane off the old Pilgrim when I'd recovered my usual sang fried.

It might be as that Warden says, all we do is hunt an fish, but as the law sharps say, "Look at the mental anguish."

National Sportsman, March 1933, 10–11

ELEVEN

The Latest from Pipestone

This piece lampoons the poor hunting and shooting skills of an inexperienced client. He fails to attain Tex's approval because he shoots the goat repeatedly after it is clearly dead. The penalty for the hunter's failure to embody proper mountain masculinity is measured by the ruined hide, "mulligan meat" (shot up too much for anything but stew, mulligatawny) and only one intact horn. The hunter has thus lost both a good trophy and the use of the meat, which contravenes a crucial part of Tex's hunting ethos.

Tex apportions some of the blame to himself, however, for having given the hunter the impression that he thought his gun, a 30.30 (a medium-calibre rifle) was not much of a "man's gun." This tips us to the fact that manhood is indeed at stake in this exercise. Revealingly, manhood turns out not to be about firepower or raw machismo—it is about skill, just measure, and restraint.

—AG

The Latest from Pipestone

———— • ————

By N. Vernon-Wood

—WB Ranch
Pipestone Creek, Alberta

Mr. John Lincoln
Wall Street. N.Y.

DEAR FRIEND,
You mind that creek that runs into the Whiterabbit from the west side? It never had a name that we knew of, except a few sort of contemperanious ones a feller thinks up while gouging through the deadfall, or side slippin on the rock.

We camped at the mouth last fall, and I'm guidin a feller thats new to this mountain stuff.

The Pilgrim was packin a 30.30, and I guess I'd give him the impressions that as a mans gun it don't rate very high in my expert opinion.

Come to think of it, the Text, firstly, thirdly, an finally of my discourse was pretty much "Bust 'em where they're biggest, knock 'em down an keep 'em down."

NEXT MORNING we get organized to give the Canadensuses hell an long about noon, we've gotten over the worst of the going. Also, we haven't seen a thing, which aint surprisin, considerin the racket we made scramblin over shale. We reaches the grass lands at last, an while takin on a load

115

of what Old Greasy alleges is bannok an cold venison, we check over the surroundin real estate with our eight powers, carefull an systematic.

The Pilgrim run true to form an located fourteen or 19 rock sheep, three four dead stump grizzly, and three snow patch goat.

We've worked down the lunch pack to what the Pilgrim called the irreducible minimum when out of a dip at the mouth of that draw, up looms a goat.

I flop onto my lunch, & the Pilgrim eases down alongside, thinking I've been took with acute gastrominous rukus, which, considerin the specific gravity of the bannok, aint surprisin. However, he is relieved when I show him the wedgeface, at the same time urging him to look as much like a columbine or skunk cabbage or something floral as possible. There aint a scrap of cover for 200 years, an why that goat aint seen us, is one of life's mysteries.

"What in hell do we do now?"

"Do nothin, just as hard as you know how, until that ol fool begins to graze, or move someplace where he aint got a goats eye view of all these Rockies," I tell him, "then belly crawl for the crick bed."

You know how damn deliberate a goat can be? Well this egg is a regular Senator, an his deliberations are right slow & ponderous. We have plenty of time to figure out what we hope to do, when, as an if we get a chance. Once we get into the creek bed we can sneak along the bank until we get to where a strip of timber comes down, & follow that up along a hogback, keepin below the crest an provided the Senator don't take it into his head to climb, we should get a shot. An remember, I wind up, a goat can shure take it, so bust him high wide an handsome.

Old whiskers, not bein in the plot remains in statue quo. Statue is right: he stands an thinks for another six hours, or anyway 20 minutes, when all of a sudden he remembers that theres a patch of perfectly splendid grass about 400 yards down—an in no time a tall he is out of sight behind the hogback, & me an the Pilgrim dash for the creek an cover.

Then come the climb. The hogback falls away in a cliff on the far side, and as I stick my face over I hear just a faint clatter of shale, & right under my nose is old Oreamnos poking along at the foot of the cliff.

I DUCK BACK an get the Pilgrim, talking with my hands like a deaf mute Sioux. We crawl to the edge again & find ourselves looking right into the Senator's face, he havin climbed some. He shure forgot his dignity that time,

116

an for a few seconds I am afraid that the Dude has got triggerfingeritis. The goat is going places with ease an celerity, when—Whammy, an down he comes, not even kickin.

Before I can open my face though, the Pilgrim lays down a barrage that 'ud stop a regiment. Five more times he killed that goat, an its not until his magazine is empty that I can convince him we have a corpus delicti.

Then I discover, that besides shootin up that goat very promiscious, he's bust him twice in the head. Even a 30.30 can do things to a trophy at about 25 yards. When the trimmin is done, we have a perforated hide, some mulligan meat, an one horn to tote to camp.

"Well you said to bust 'em didnt you" is all the satisfaction I get.

Anyway, when you want to refer to that creek that runs into the Whiterabbit from the west, remember its now Bustum Creek.

Yours truly,

Tex.

Hunting and Fishing, February 1934, 11

TWELVE

DRIED SPINACH OR MOOSE STEAK?

The story ends with regret for killing a moose that was a favoured pet (and money maker) for an aristocratic hotelier—for whom Tex has nothing but scorn. This is part of a conscious attempt by Tex to distance himself from the effete aristocratic whims and airs of a Marquis who ran a lodge near Banff and refused to let anyone hunt on the territory he leased. Tex refers to his friends and himself as "waddies," "proletariat," and "commoners." They are the ones who have to rally round if there is a problem, but otherwise they keep a "respectful distance." The tone of regret at the end (and the use of words like "old reactionaries") suggests a more gentle character and sensibility than does the belligerent populist tone he strikes at the beginning.

—AG

Dried Spinach or Moose Steak?

———— • ————

By N. Vernon-Wood

From the Bar WB Outfit, Pipestone Creek, Alberta; to Mr. John Lincoln, Wall Street, New York:

Dear Friend:

You've heard 47 different varieties of that yarn where the guy shoots the farmer's cow in mistake for a deer, an' I guess like me you thought that a bird who'd make a boner like that should see a specialist. Well, I hate to admit it, but I come awful close to gettin' elected to that club myself.

Last summer, we accumulated another tenderfoot trap in these here hills. It ain't the usual Dude Ranch deadfall, but just a mess of log cabins by a lake, with a couple of snow peaks in the door yard. It's run an' owned by an honest to gosh Marquis, with all the frills of a shootin' box in the Tyroll, an 'the deft an sophisticated service"—see advts.—"of a Ducal country home."

Natchelly there ain't any place in this scheme for uncouth waddies like Sawback, or me an Jim, so when we have to infest that part of the country, we camp at a respectful distance.

Bout the only times the Markee deigns to be aware of our existence is when his pack string strays, or a couple of his victims get bushed. Then the proletariat are expected to dash madly about, an give a good imitation of the faithful varlets strivin right mightily to discover My Lord his palfreys.

We done it, too, not because we are so neighborly with the aristocracy, but because old Sawback Smith is hired to wrangle, pack, guide, an as general

121

factotum. While he's a top hand, the noble employer finds so many side lines for Sawback to tend to while he's restin, we sort of feel it's up to the commoners to rally round, an not let the Baron get the idee that his man has bit off more than he can chew. On top of that, there's a right attractive filly holdin down the kitchen at the camp, an the boys ain't adverse to bein invited to surround a cup of coffee an a wedge of pie before hittin the trail back.

Dave White (Airtights, Gents Furnishin, Hardware, Feed, Harness, and Insurance) shure does a land office business in silk neckerchiefs an ice cream shirts last summer.

Me, I ain't all het up with enthusiasm about this new spread. The Duke has planted his snare plumb in the middle of a patch of country I'm in the habit of harassin durin the huntin season. He's got a lease on a township, an is one of these here little brothers of the birds an beasts. While I'm in line with a reasonable amount of conservation, an dead agin killin just to see a beast fall over, I'm also one of the old reactionaries who still figger that game was put in the mountains to provide huntin for men, an mebbe the odd woman. I can't see eye to eye with the Markee when, as Sawback tells me, he won't even bump off the saddle chewin porcupine or haze the bears who bust open the meat house ever so often.

The word goes forth that there's to be no assault, mayhem, or battery committed on any bird, beast, or fish whatsoever on the Duckal domain.

Last fall, I'm on my way to the forks of the Cross, an make camp about a mile from this Ki Wet Tin Ok Camp, as it's called.

That evenin Sawback drifted over, to hear some talk that wasn't all cluttered up with French, Latin, Oxford English, an Back Bay American.

Durin the gab fest he tells about a bull moose that's sort of the star attraction over to the Chalet. He's got a taste of salt, at the horse lick, an acquired a likin for spud peelins an such. The dudes spent time an miles of fillum takin his picture, an all in all he's worth quite a price on the hoof to the Markee as a adjunct to the free life of the Far West.

Accordin to Sawback, he's a roan. You see 'em fairly frequent, a sort of blue roan that's right pretty. They ain't so scarce as to be all hopped up about, though.

I thought Sawback looked kinda peeked, an after a while he come out with the reason. A bear has raided the meat house again an the camp is on a diet of dried spinach, powdered eggs, an beans.

"I ain't throwed my lip over a hunk of beef, pork, or sow belly this two weeks," he says, "an pretty soon I'll be turnin myself out to graze with the rest of the cayuses."

I'm movin camp a few miles down next day, an figger to start huntin just as soon as I am offen the Markee's pet game preserve, so I tell Sawback that, if I can get any meat, I'll let him know an he can ride over an snare him a quarter. All I need is enough red steak to do me till I get to the forks, where I hope to bust a sheep. An I'd ruther masticate mountain sheep than anything I know of.

Next evenin, I'm sneakin around the shore of Wedgwood Lake, and just as it's gettin dusk I spot a moose crossin the shallows at the far end. I wait until he is out of the drink, and plaster him. Openin him up to cool, I leave him lay, an next day I send the wrangler hightailin back to the Duke's, with word for Sawback to grab him a pack pony an rally round the meat market.

By noon we are at my kill, an when the old waddie sees it he let out a whistle.

"Feller, you don it," he says. "By the woolly hind quarters of Astor's pet goat, that's the Markee's blue moose. Man, oh, man, if he ever gets onto this he'll have you racked, thumscrewed, burnt an quartered, an flung into the moat, not to mention pinched, unfrocked, struck offen the rolls, an excommunicated."

"Aw, coil your rope," I tell him. "You or your princely employer can't tell the color of a beast's hide from the gravy. Load your bronk, an if His Serenity wants to keep his damn pets sacrosanct, let him bell 'em, or fence 'em."

Just the same, I did feel some egregious.

THANKS FOR THE MAGAZINES an newspapers. Last winter, we was stormbound so much that I learnt all of the Stockman's Almanac by heart, an most of the Government's report on grasshopper control. I sure was pinin for a change of thought.

—Yours truly, TEX.

Hunting and Fishing, June 1935, 11

THIRTEEN

Tex Reads His Permit

Tex has only scorn for the new class of local functionary with a university education, such as the Park Warden, and is scathing in his dismissal of the sorts of things they would learn in university programs devoted to "Silviculture, Sikology, Practical Prospectin', an' Needlepoint Embroidery" ("Tex Reads his Permit"). The book-learned Warden he encounters does not disappoint: he is an incompetent woodsman, all officiousness, and condescending to boot; in the story, Tex mixes it up with him on account of disrespectful comments. Interestingly, it's not book-learning per se that Tex abominates—after all, he clearly had a fair amount of it himself. Rather, the new disciplines being taught at university attract his ridicule, as much for their own sake as for their utter uselessness for a Park Warden, at least in those days—silviculture might come in handy today, though psychology will not be any better now than it was then.

This story is the only one to directly discuss Tex's long association with the Walcotts, and he mentions them only because the "poaching" within Park boundaries is for them and the Smithsonian. He guards himself very carefully against name-dropping, remarkable for a man who had worked on Hollywood films, both in Banff and in California, as an animal handler (for instance, on *Call of the Wild*, 1935), and had a bevy of illustrious clients.

—AG

TEX READS HIS PERMIT

———————— • ————————

A Pipestone Letter—
By N. Vernon-Wood

From the Bar WB Outfit, Pipestone Creek, Alberta; to Mr. John Lincoln,
Wall Street, New York:

DEAR FRIEND:
It's a long time that I don't take my pen in hand and give you the dope on
the happenings up an' down the Pipestone. Well, life goes on, as the feller
says, and most of us are makin' out to eat three–four times a day, though I
got it figgered that when the new game warden sort of gets onto the ropes
some of the boys will have to cut down on out-of-season venison.

This new warden is one of those sikological experiments, or whatever
you call 'em. Seems like the Game Commission took an hour or so off from
the multitudinfarious duties such as speakin' at Fishin' Society dinners,
Skeet Club suppers, and etc., tellin' all an' sundry what they were gettin
ready to consider startin' mebbe to make Alberta the Sportsman's Paradise.
Regrettin' meantime that owein' to the current financial flacidity the price
of fishin' licenses would be boosted a buck, game ditto two bucks, with a
reduction on the bag an' a two-inch increase in the legal length of trout.

The game laws are gettin' some complicated an' I'm waiverin' between
retaining council or just interpretin' them my own way. However, to get back
to the trail, the commission opined that the old-fashioned ex-lumberjack,
ex-cowhand, ex-trapper, was out as warden material. Anyway they figger
them natural produks of the soil are too sympathetik in their idees with

the hoi polloi they are suppose to check up on. Also an' moreover, we got a perfectly good University that teaches Silviculture, Sikology, Practical Prospectin', an' Needlepoint Embroidery, so, let's appoint a flock of scientific wardens, who ain't got any entanglin' alliances with them poachin' so-an-so's in the mountains.

This also has the advantage of findin' jobs for several of the sons of our local legislature, who have been educated all to hell but haven't yet been able to get absorbed into the professions.

Motion carried, the Hon. Ike Ruttle only dissentin'. His family bein' all gals.

The first of these erudite birds is appointed to the Pipestone district last summer. I don't run into him when he makes his first patrol, so don't meet him social or official until fall.

I got me a job with a museum outfit to help collect a few fauna while a couple of professors specialize on flora an' fossils. We got a permit from the Govt. to take two males an' one female of any species whatsoever, anywhere, anytime. In fact we got the whole country on a platter.

Four days after leavin' the home place we was camped at the foot of Badger Pass. While my Pilgrims are runnin' down Trilobites an' Saxifrages, I take me a scout up on the summit. The country is crummy with Bighorn, an' for years I've wanted a chance to take a poke at a couple of 'em. Bein' a game reserve, them rams got plumb highty-tighty. They'd stand on a ledge an' not even pay you the compliment of lookin' scared, an' I shure did pine to teach 'em respect. Here's my one chance, an' I'm takin' my time an' makin' it last.

As I was checkin' over the terra firma, I seen a couple of cayuses 'way down on the other side of the pass, an' the glasses showed one hombre an' a pack pony makin' a pretty poor stab at findin' the trail over. I wasn't particularly interested, an' confined my attention to a flock of *Ovis canadenses* that was just figuratively fingerin' their noses at me. One of 'em looked like he'd show up noble in a glass case so I bust him, an' proceeded to take the 47 different measurements the museum opined they needed. Every so often, I'd fill the pipe an' take a look down the pass to see if the bird with the pack horse was comin' or goin'.

'Bout the time I've got my specimen all ready to lug into camp he is showin' up, an' I think, if he's any kind of a man, he'll pack my plunder on his pony into camp for me. I was settin' by the trail feelin' at peace with all mankind when he rides up.

128

"Whereinhell is the trail over this pass?" is his greetin'. "I've been two days trying to find it."

Then he sort of noticed my layout.

"AHAH!" he says, "Poachin,' what? Gimme that rifle. Don't you know it's illegal to carry arms in the game reserve?"

"Yeah, I knowed it when you was still wearin' didies," I tell him.

"So. Deliberate infraction of the regulations made an' provided. Where are you camped, what's your name, are you alone?" An' a whole lot more.

"I'm camped a couple miles down the valley," I tell him, "but don't go off half-cocked. I'm Tex Wood, an' I'm with the Museum outfit, an' I got a special dispensation from Geo. Rex to collect."

"How do I know you're Wood?" he says, "have you your permit with you? You will come along with me. Leave that ram there until I come back and take photographs for evidence agen you."

"How do I know you're a warden? You talk like a preacher to me, an' you might have gotten that tin badge out of a popcorn packet," I tell him, gettin' some het up.

He fished out a flock of papers an' showed me his commission, an' 27 other credentials.

"All right," I say, "I'll go along peaceable, but I'll pack my rifle, I think a heap of that old tool an' don't trust it with no strangers or children."

"All right, you keep ahead of me, and no funny work, my man."

So we start to backtrack. They was a mud slide over the trail just at the foot of the shale, an' I start over, bein' careful to step where I'd have fairly good footin'. I am only about twenty feet along when my herder bogs down good an' proper. His pack pony is up to the cinch buckles, an' his saddle horse damn near out of sight. I put in quite a pleasant half hour watchin' a demonstration of how not to extricate a couple of knotheads from a mud hole. I reckon that ain't a required course up at dear old Whoosis, an' the game laws don't say anythin' about a poacher havin' to assist a warden. Anyhow, I'm plum legal an' legitimate, an' takin' all the good I can out of it.

When we finally get into camp, my two companions in the pursuit of knowledge are in, checkin' over their day's takin's. The Warden sort of recognizes them as kindred spirits, an' enters into a long an' mighty authoritative dissertation on the wherefores of Brachipods. When I get a chance to put a spoke in edgeways, I suggest, plum respectful, that he look over my permit.

"Oh, don't bother," he says, "I expect you are bono fidee, although you don't look it."

He was a pretty husky young feller, an' he never did read the permit. By the time I'd got him where he was willin' to listen to reason, I was settin' on his head, an' the document was kind of wore out, so I just read it to him between rounds.

Well, the geese will be comin' north mighty soon. Why don't you follow a good example, an' come up too?

—Yours truly,

Tex.

Hunting and Fishing, August 1935, 13

FOURTEEN

THE GUIDE KNOWS EVERYTHING

The tender tone of this late story is quite different from the rough-and-tumble of such earlier pieces as "The Last Buffalo Drive," with its coarse and violent mischief. Tex's regard for Father Moriarty shows that although hunting or fishing prowess was a crucial requisite of true mountain masculinity, ethical qualities and practices were equally important, and perhaps too an appreciation of philosophical and religious values (at least as they applied to animals): Tex cites with quiet approval and no irony the Father's Platonic or rather neo-Thomist sermon to the fish he releases. The core values of Tex's mountain masculinity are emphasized by the contrast between the priest's body ("a paunchy little priest") and his gentleness ("gentle as a woman") and his ability with a fly and a rod. The literary allusions to the fisherman apostles, Izaak Walton's *The Compleat Angler* and Grey of Fallodon's *Fly Fishing*[1] once again betray the broad reading and culture of the author. The story lampoons the tendency of guides to think or behave as if they know everything, ending with another tender moment between Tex and his son Bill.

—AG

---

1. Edward Grey, First Viscount Grey of Fallodon, published *Fly-Fishing* (London: Dent and Sons, 1899) in the British Empire, then in the United States under the title *Recreation* (Boston: Houghton Mifflin and Company, 1920).

The Guide Knows Everything

———— • ————

By N. Vernon-Wood

THREE–FOUR YEARS AGO, the Trail Riders of the Canadian Rockies had a picture in their bulletin that shure give us local dude wranglers a kick. It's a photo of old Bill Slaney conversin' with a bevy of sweet young she-Pilgrims. The old side-hill gouger is looking plumb intelligent (for him), an' it's titled "The Guide Knows Everything."

Which same is ondoubtedly what some Pilgrims seem to expect. A man's got to know the country, an' how to make a comfortable camp. He has to be able to shoe a cayuse, patch a tent, swing an ax, an' build a decent meal; an' when he can do them he's only just started. He mighty soon discovers that he also has to be a naturalist, geologist, an' botanist, besides a jack-knife surgeon, a recontoor, a ballistics expert, an' a pretty fair judge of human nature an' how much exposure to give a fillum on a dull day.

An' every once in a while some bird will pull something like this: "Look at that view, Tex; don't you think Corot would have loved to paint it, or do you think Browning would have caught the atmosphere better—or do you?"

When they start that sort of thing, it's a good plan to grab your field glasses plumb excited an' say, "Holy old doodle, they's a bear on that slide—no, b'gosh, it's a burned stump. Don't it beat hell how them shadders fool you sometimes?"

ALL THIS HERE PREAMBLE is by way of explainin' why it is a feller's apt to get him what the experts call a Complex. He gets so he begins to think he

133

just about does know it all, an' just then somethin' sneaks up an' busts his little pink balloon all to hell.

Take trout fishin, f'rinstance. I'm what you might call a fair-to-middlin' journeyman angler, but most of my stream whippin' has been done for strictly utilitarian purposes, fish in the pan bein' the prime motive, an' I've never branched out into the finer an' more artistic aspects of the sport. But that don't prevent me recognizin' an' appreciatin' a top hand when I see one. An' Father Moriarty was one of 'em. He's the priest in charge of the Bankhead Mission, an' shepherd to the wildest flock of woolies that ever cracked a prayer-book.

I'm comin' down Johnson Canyon, onetime, an' down at the bottom of a cliff, in a scrub spruce, I find a hummin'-bird's nest—one of them delicate bits of ornithological construction that makes a man feel clumsy as an ox, just to look at. I meet up with this Padre, who has a camera an' fishin' rod along with him, so I ask does he want to make a picture of the nest, with a cute ruby-throat settin' on a couple of pea-sized eggs. Right away he got human, an' we scrambled back together.

From bird's-nesting with a camera we naturally got on to fishin', an' I took the old feller to the pool at the foot of the falls. That hole was one of the major blights in my comparatively carefree existence. It's full of rainbow trout as big as pack horses, almost, an' are they snooty? I've tried 'em with Royal Coachmen, Brown Hackles, an' Black Gnats accordin' to season an' weather conditions. I've used Bucktails, Colorado Spinners, Rubber Grasshoppers, an' God help me, worms. The mornin' sun has risen on my shiverin' form, up to my pants pockets in the icy water, tryin' to inviggle them blasted 'bows to strike, an' it's gone down behind Sawback Peak throwin' its last crimson beam on a disgruntled waddy still feebly castin' along the edge of the riffles. An' all I ever took out of there was half a dozen tiddlers that was too immature to know better.

I led his Reverence to that hole with malice aforethought. I'd got the notion that if I couldn't catch them trout, no one could—same bein' a typical example of Guide Philosophy.

His eyes kind of lit up when we looked down into the drink, an' he says, "What do you suggest we use?"

"Well," I tell him. "I think I'll try a Wickham's Fancy as a dropper, an' a Gnat for point. What flies you got?"

"I think I'll just sit and watch a while. I'm not as young as I was, and a rest seems to be indicated."

134

So I unwound a leader from my hat, an' unlimbered my rod. I've got to let on that I really believe them pediculous pink-bellies are takeable, but it's just a gesture as far's I'm concerned. The Father sat him on a rock, an' seemed about as interested as a river hog at a ladies' quiltin' bee. After I'd made forty-'leven fruitless casts, he pulled a mess of feathers, yarn, horsehair, an' old socks out of his pocket, an' opened a tin that had originally contained half a pound of Dublin Shag. Out come a few hooks, a pair of scissors, an' he went to work.

A few minutes later, he stepped up alongside an' laid seventy foot of line across that pool in a manner that was a joy to see. He's usin' only one fly, an' it lit like thistle-down on the lee side of a big rock that stuck out where the water boiled after plunging over the falls.

Just as he recovered, I thought I seen a shadowy shape, rise, an' on the next cast I knew it. It come up from behind that rock, an' struck like the trip-hammers of hell. An' I stood an' watched a paunchy little priest handle six an' one-half pounds of wet dynamite an' lightnin' with a four-ounce rod in a manner that got me thinkin' of D'Artagnan, an' the swordsman's wrist. What's more, I found out later he uses a leader like cobweb.

That little man could sit on the bank of a stream, study the water, weather, an' the insect life, an' then take somethin' from his fly-book that would look to those trout the way fresh-broiled deer liver looks to a hungry Pilgrim. I got so I invented jobs over to Bankhead on the off chance of runnin' into Father Moriarty an' persuadin' him to play hookey. I've seen him catch trout where there wasn't any, an' I never seen him lift more'n two out of the water in any one day. He'd bring 'em to the shallows, slip his fingers down the line an' takin' care his hand was wet, slip out his hook gentle as a woman. "There you are," he'd say. "Back to your pet eddy, an' meditate on the sin of gluttony, an' next time, don't mistake the shadow for the substance."

They buried the Father last fall. From the cemetery here, you can hear the Bow falls roarin' loud an' deep in the spring, an' sort of musical the rest of the time, so his body is right handy to good trout water, an' I'll bet you four fits that his spirit is havin' one whale of a time with them other sportsmen, the Galilee fishermen, Ike Walton, an' Grey of Falloden.

LAST FALL, HAVIN' NOTHIN' much to do, an' a month to do it in, I says to the youngest of my quiverful, "Want to skip school an' come along with me while I see can we get the odd elk for eatin' purposes, son?"

135

Which is Unnecessary Question No. 59. So we pack a couple of cayuses an' hit south. Three days' travel puts us at the foot of a pass that divides Alberta from British Columbia, an' is the watershed between the Saskatchewan an' Columbia river systems. The B.C. side is crummy with elk, an' there's bear on both slopes. We fixed up camp for a week's stay, an' next mornin' headed up the pass afoot. Before we'd gone three miles, we'd spotted nine bulls, mostly young stuff, an' all easy pickin's.

The kid wanted we should bust the first one we seen, but I thought this was as good a time as any to inculcate a little hunter's patience into his system.

"No hurry, son; never grab the first thing you see, when you might get just what you want later."

Couple of hours after, we spotted a twelve-pointer 'way up on a slide, so we made a stalk, an' laid him out. I grallocked him, an' takin' only the liver for immediate consumption, hung my old sweater on his antlers to flag off the prowlin' coyote, an' we backtracked for camp.

While we're fryin' up some liver next mornin', the youngster want to know was there any trout in the crick that wandered by camp.

"Search me, son," I says, "but I doubt it. It's a right pifflin' watercourse, an' I never took the trouble to wet a line in it. Still an' all, trout, like God, are where you find 'em. Want to take a whirl at it?"

He opined he might, so I tell him to get the tackle an' go to it, while I salvage the meat. I figger it's a good way to keep him occupied while I tend to the serious business of life. What with this an' that, I don't get back till mid-afternoon. There's no sign of his Nibs in camp, so after hanging the plunder over a smudge to discourage the flies, I wander downstream to see has a grizzly spooked him into a tree, or is he asleep on the bank.

Half a mile below camp, I meet him ploddin' along. Ploddin' is right! He's wet, cold an' hungry, but is he downhearted? The peaks echo "no!" The little sonofagun has a mess of cutthroat, runnin' from four to six pounds apiece, that any man would be proud of.

After we'd fed our faces, an' admired them trout some, he says, "Dad, did you know there was trout like that in this crick?"

"Son, I didn't know they was anything more than frogs, an' that's a fact."

He gives me one of them, long, cold looks that kids can turn on so good. "Heck," he says, "I thought you guides knowed everythin'."

National Sportsman, June 1936, 14–15

FIFTEEN

Tex: Gentleman's Gentleman

This story, published in August 1936, parallels the tale of outrageous laxity and lack of mountain masculinity Tex finds in the two British aristocrats in "William, Prepare my Barth" (*The Sportsman,* July 1930). In fact, the stories are close enough for this one to be a repetition of the other. The two hunters commit every imaginable sin against mountain masculinity: they dress too colourfully and too fashionably; they rise late; they wash and shave and dress carefully; they want to hunt on horseback, not climbing up and down mountains; they do not abide by sporting rules—one tells how he shot a sitting grouse through the roof of a tent—and finally, sin of sins, they refuse to get wet or dirty, thus destroying their chances of bagging any game and redeeming themselves.

—AG

Tex: Gentleman's Gentleman

————————— • —————————

A Pipestone Letter
By N. Vernon-Wood

—*WB Ranch*
Pipestone Creek, Alberta

Mr. John Lincoln
Wall Street, N.Y.

Dear Friend:

There's been a whole lot of water gone over the Bow falls since I wrote you last, but you know how it is. Just about the time I'm ready to take pen in hand an' inflict a mess of local gossip on you, some bird comes down the trail with a cayuse to trade, or mebbe the pasture fence needs fixin', or the venison's gettin' low. By the time a man's caught up on them chores he's wore out & has to recuperate, so he wrestles a couple of broncs and takes a sashay over the Pass to see how the Elk crop's doin', or is the hoss feed any good.

Now I got all kinds of sympathy for blokes that are always findin' excuses for not doin' such extranious things as shavin', writin' letters, or washin' dishes, but when it comes to the serious business of Life, like huntin' & fishin'—when a guy dallies around, he's got me beat.

Me an' Sawback Smith, we're willin' to guide 'most any variety of Pilgrim that buys R.R. tickets to these parts, an' can usually point out a Elk or a Goat that's honin' to get busted with lead. But when it comes to actin' as a gentleman's personal gentleman to a coupla fashion-plate Pilgrims who are so bloomin' equestrian they can't get off their knotheads long enough to eat, we don't do so good.

Like last Fall. Sawback an' me sold ourselves down the river to a pair of Dudes who aimed to tangle with a flock of Grizzly, Elk, Deer, Side-hill Gougers, Pinto Cayuses, & other Western fauna. Me & him are down at the deepo when the Trans Canada come in, waitin' to pick up our Pilgrims an' incidental to get a eyeful of the youth & beauty from Massachusetts, Sutton Place, an' Bailey's Beach who are headin' for the rustic comforts of the big hotel.

I'm tryin' to look plumb sang froid as I hear a pippin say to her buddy, "Look at that perfeckly delightful cow person, Madge!" when Sawback jabs his elbow clear up to the shoulder into my quiverin' diagram. "D'yuh see what I see?" he sez.

Comin' up the platform are a pair of sports that for sartorial munificence have got Mrs. Astor's plush goat lookin' like a grizzled section hand. They're the combined produck of the leadin' fashion pages, a Bond Street tailor, an' untrammeled imagination. It's a symphony of checked mackinaw in the pastel shades—Red, Yeller, Green, with an over-check of Royal Purple. I'm lost complete in wonder & amazement an' don't notice, till I hear Sawback cussin', that they're totin' gun cases. It seems that these are our huntin' buddies for the follerin' two weeks, God help us!

For the next couple of days, while we're trailin' out to the game country, we're sizin' each other up. I notice that when them dudes tell their huntin' experiences they bear down heavy on the fact that they rode up on their game. Now, I got nothin' against hosses, but there's a heap of places in these hills where a cayuse is just another unnecessity, an' there's lots of times you have to tie him to a tree while you stalk afoot. Then you see somethin' interestin' up & over, or 'way down agen, but you can't carry on because you've got to retrieve dobbin.

One of these Pilgrims tells what he alleges is a humorous story.

He's on a huntin' trip, an' one AM is layin' in his flea bag when a Grouse perches on the tent roof. All he can see through the canvas is the print of the bird's feet, so he reaches stealthily for his fowlin' piece and blasts that fool hen from the inside, thereby qualifyin' for the Shootem Sittin' Club, an' providin' a problem in needlework for his guide an' mentor, who likely had to sacrifice his shirt tail to patch the rag house.

Funny, huh? Like hell; but it gives me a line on that bird's habits & disposition. It turned plenty cold before we hit the huntin' camp, but there was two-three inches of fresh trackin' snow that made us feel good. On the way down to the crick next mornin' I run across a fresh set of Grizzly tracks, so cuttin' the mattutinal absolutions short, I gallop for the tent to stir up the Dudes. I expect 'em to come boilin' out like a fire department. Instead, one sez, "Okay. You go an' get the saddle hosses while we shave an' have breakfast."

"But it'll take mebbe two hours to find the knotheads, an' even then we can't make walkin' time in this mess of deadfall," I tell him.

Right away one Pilgrim decides he ain't lost any Grizzly, and rolls over for another bout with Morpheus. I coax the other into his purple an' fine linen, an' stand around while he scrapes his face, manicures his nails, an' tonics his hair. He dallies with his bacon & flap-jacks, an' at long last we get goin'.

Instead of splashin' through the crick, which is all of four inches deep, he wanders up & down the bank lookin' for a log to cross on. When he found one, he got halfway across an' fell off. His mackinaw britches are all of a half inch thick, but there's a cupful of water splashed on 'em, so he returns to camp to break out another pair, an' that finishes that hunt. An' I've guided female women who've jumped into a glacier-fed crick up to their shirt pockets to bring a trout to net!

THE CLIMAX COME about a week later. Our Pilgrims ain't fired a shot yet, Elk and what-not bein' unaddicted to perchin' on tent roofs.

Sawback comes boilin' out of their wickiup, where he has been in conference. The Pilgrims have been tryin' to persuade him to hunt Elk on alder slides by hossback—them slides bein' navigable only by a man who's willin' to wear out his vest crawlin'. Sawback dashes over to where I'm watchin' a pair of Bulls, about a thousand feet above camp, an' blurts: "I'm through—*feenee*," he sez. "There's them two resplendent hot-house producks layin' in bed with their sweaters & coats on, an' wooley caps over their ears, tellin' *me* how to hunt."

Which is just about as reasonable as me tryin' to tell a Antelope how to run.

If I can't figger a good alibi, I'll be writin' you agen.

Yours truly,

TEX.

Hunting and Fishing, August 1936, 14

SIXTEEN

IT'S GOOD TO BE ALIVE

The language in this story gives the author away as a man who attended a Latin school: Tex uses words like "Ol' Sol," "sextenarians," "celerious," "matutinal," and "vespers" that have Latin origins; yet he also mixes in outright malapropisms like "perpendiculous" and "phenominum," and deliberate misspellings ("beautious"), so as not to look overly educated and too much like the elitist clients he heartily disliked.

Here as elsewhere, Tex articulates his philosophy of hunting: it's fine to kill an animal, but only if you are going to use as much of it as you can, not just the head and skin for trophies.

Although the client makes a bit of a fool of himself, at least he admits it. A terrifying episode puts things into perspective: Tex's mild annoyance at the client's comfortable philosophizing about the wonderful day turns into agreement by nightfall, after they both have a close shave.

—AG and JR

IT'S GOOD TO BE ALIVE

———————— • ————————

By N. Vernon-Wood

IT LOOKS LIKE ANOTHER one of them swell days when Ol' Sol pokes his snoot over the mounting an' says Good Morning all over our camp. It's Indian Summer, an' there's a smell in the air that sort of makes yore hair bristle, an' you want to go out an' slap a Grizzly's face just to see if he's got nerve enough to do something about it.

At least, it seems to affect my Pilgrim that way. He's sittin' cross-laigged by the fire, scalin' flapjacks down as fast as Greasy can slide 'em off'n the skillet, an' breathin' deep of the mornin' ozone like he was takin' exercises.

"Tex," says this Pilgrim around the edge of a flapjack, "you know it's worth five hundred Gold Standard dollars, just to be alive this morning."

Which is his way of lookin' at it. There's a blister on my heel, left over from scalin' a few thousand perpendiculous feet of slides the day previous; I got a hangnail that don't feel so good, an' besides, I'm not addicted to deep breathin' of a mornin', so I just grunts. Bein' alive don't seem any better today than it did yesterday, an' yesterday I found the beginnin' of a crack in the stock of my favorite rifle.

"Mebbe," I growls, thinkin' of the blister an' the crack, "but I druther see the five hundred."

ME AN' THE PILGRIM got going right celerious after breakfast, an' high-tailed for the slides, an' the general direction of a Wapiti we'd heard trumpetin' earlier in the mornin'. By ten o'clock the Ol' Haymaker has melted the frost, an' it's warm enough to peel off our sweaters. There ain't a mosquito

145

or hoss fly in six townships, an' on the slides the huckleberries are thick as sextenarians at a Townsend picnic. We're depletin' the visible supply when that Elk let out a holler so close I thought he was in my pocket. The Pilgrim grabbed his rifle, an' we both looked in fourteen different directions, when I caught the glint of sun on the ivory-white tips of his antlers, an' silently pointed.

As we watched, the Elk stalked out into the open, an' I begun to laff. It's a young Bull of eight points, narrow in the spread, an' right spindley in the beam, but man, oh man, has he a voice? To hear him, you'd think he rated a fifty-inch spread an' fourteen points. Which, when you come to think of it, is another point of similarity between us sapiens an' the rest of the mammalia.

So leavin' almighty-voice to accumulate years an' spikes, we oozed along, up an' on, over scree slopes, around scrub balsam patches, an' through larch groves. We're settin' on an outcrop, catchin' up our wind, an' watchin' for somethin' to show up; way below us, Leman Lake looked like a big turquoise layin' on green velvet, an' here an' there, the golden brown of the slide grass run up to the silver gray of the limestone. The Pilgrim is takin' on somethin' epic about Nature's Canvas, an' the color harmony of Sky, Lake, an' Forest, when I seen somethin' that made me jab my elbow into his ribs, shuttin' off the flow of rhetoric.

Standin' out on a two-bit bench about three hundred yards away, an' slightly downhill, is a perfectly good Elk. He's as still as a bronze image an' watchin' somethin'. Then I see, way down in the crick bottom, a half-dozen cows pokin' along footloose an' fancy free.

The question immediately arises will we take a poke at him right now, or shall we try to stalk closer, meantime runnin' the chance of his decidin' to constitute himself a welcomin' committee of one, an' go tearin' down to thrill them females.

A bird I'm guidin' one time promulgates the theory that a successful hunter has to try to think like he thinks the beast he's huntin' thinks. If you get what I mean.

So, I think—here I am, a right personable batchelor Wapiti, with plenty free time and no place special to go, and yonder's a bunch of beautious gals, down there by the crick. An' I see myself tearin' down the slide, knockin' over some right sizeable timber in my onseemly haste—so I says to the Pilgrim, "About three hundred an' don't forget it's a downhill shot, so aim low."

IT'S A SHAME to nip romance before it's budded, but we need that trophy, an' the .30-06 Springfield, with a certain amount of co-operation from my Dude, done it.

"An' now," I says, "you can turn loose your flow of declamation relatin' to nature's palette all you like, while I perform several major operations on that beast."

There's a heap of awful good chewin' on a Elk, an' when it comes to salvagin' meat, I'm a reg'lar Indian. Nothin' burns me up like the eggs who drop a prime animal, an' then just saw offen the head, an' leave the meat for the Coyotes an' Wolverines. By the time I've dessected the kill, an' hung up the steaks an' roasts to cool, the shadows are gettin' long.

I got the head on my shoulders, an' we hit for the valley. There ain't any trail, so I'm watchin' my footin', an' not payin' any attention to what's goin' on elsewhere. The Pilgrim bein' burdened only with the liver an' a couple of back strips, is checkin' over the slides, an' suddenly says, "Tex, I'd swear there's a Bear on the second opening to the left."

I dropped the Elk head, glad of the chance, an' fished my binoculars out of my shirt front. "Yeah—it's a Bear all right all right," I said after a look. "Either a fair Black or a small Grizzly—wait until he turns—yeah, it's a Grizzly, but he ain't such a much."

"He looked big to me," says the Pilgrim. "Are you sure you're lookin' in the right place?"

"Well, I'm lookin' at a Bear, but from where I stand, he don't look like any rug for your liberry. He might make a couple pair of fur-lined garters for a small chorus gal," I reply. "What you want to do—go get him or leave him lay?"

"Let's stalk it anyway."

So I hung the Elk head in a spruce, an' we started to climb, anglin' toward the second slide. When we got to the edge of the timber we snuck up, an' checked over the open slopes. Nothin' in sight, up, down or across. What to do? Go higher, or slip down keepin' in cover of the trees? I'm all for the latter for various reasons, the main one bein' that it's in the general direction of camp, an' them matutinal flapjacks an' bacon have long ago been burnt up producin' energy for luggin' twelve-point Elk heads over the surroundin' terrain. But I bluff the Dude that it's logical for a Bear to travel downhill for evenin' vespers.

147

AT THAT, I'M RIGHT. We hadn't gone five hundred yards when we seen a clump of willow bush wavin' to an' fro, with no wind to agitate it. Somepin' in it, shure as hell is a man trap. Before I could spit, the bear showed part of him clear, and the Pilgrim cut loose. At the second shot Bruin come out of the bush, half rollin' an' half runnin'. Whammy—the Springfield sings out agen, an' the Bear flopped an' stayed put. We eased up, careful to see was he out, or just playin' possum until we was in rushin' distance.

It's a small Grizzly, an' not much of a trophy, as trophies go, altho' I've seen smaller ones that left this part of God's country addressed to the Taxidermist.

The Dude is feelin' kinda six-for-a-nickel. He looks at the Bear kinda thoughtful, an' says, "How wouldja like a new rug for the livin' room floor?"

I see what he's drivin' at, so I says as nonchalant as hell, "My missus asked me to accumulate some kinda hide to cover the hole in the livin' room rug, an' this'll just about fit. Tell you what. While I go to work on this schoolboy, you amble back to camp with the liver an' tell ol' Greasy that I'll be 'bout half an hour behind you, an' that about a pound of liver cut thick, rolled in cornmeal, an' fried not too much in deep fat, with a side order of fool-hen, a quart of java, an' plenty boiled rice an' raisins is what my system craves."

I guess the Pilgrim was lookin' for an excuse to fade from the scene of his infanticide, because he didn't even argue.

It's dusk by the time I am ready to hit for camp. I'd left the head in the hide, figurin' to skin that out in camp. I shoved the works into my rucksack an' began movin'. When I got to the foot of the slide, it was dark.

DID YOU EVER have that spooky feelin' that somebody or something is doggin' you? Most generally, I've got the nervous temperament of a mud turtle, but somehow that evenin' I don't feel as placid as usual. Then I heard a faint snap behind me, like somethin' broke a small twig. I turned, quick, an' man of man, I felt my heart jar my bridgework.

Not twenty feet behind me was a real Grizzly. It was nine feet high an' twenty-four feet long, an' three ax handles an' a plug of eatin' tobacco between the eyes. Anyhow, that's how it looked first time. When I turned, it stopped an' just set.

"An' now what?" I thought. I ain't got any rifle, an' somehow I can't see myself engagin' hand to hand with a Grizzly b'ar.

Men an' bretherin, I'm here to tell you that the hardest thing I ever did in forty-odd misspent years, was to turn my back on that Horribilis, an' go down the trail, trying' to kid myself that calmness an' coolness was the ticket. I'm tryin' to make that Bear believe that havin' him tag me along was nothin' onusual, an' that blame thing done just that. Ever' so often I'd take a quick look behind, an' there it'd be, two jumps behind, an' still comin'. I expect to feel his teeth in my off ear any minute. I wonder if it's the mother of the precocious adolescent I've got on my back, an' if so, just when she'd decide to work me over, or is it just another Bear that's mebbe attracted by the phenominum of perfectly good Bear smell all mixed up with man-scent. It's a academic question that I druther was more hypothetical right now. All I know is, the only Bears I'm goin' to like from now on are those that are laid out, harmless an' tee-totally defunct, an' ready for the skinnin' knife.

I wanted like hell to run, but what's the use? The Bear can overtake me in three jumps, an' anyhow it's no sign of a gentleman to be in a hurry. I want to shout, but my mouth an' throat is dry as the Mojave Desert. I'm shiverin' an' sweatin' an' cussin' an' wishin' I knew more prayers.

When we finally got to where the crick we'd been followin' run into the river, it's a leetle lighter. The valley is more open, an' the stars are out, an' I think how peaceful an' safe-life the crick looked when we forded it a few days back.

I take another quick look behind an' see the Bear, still on my trail. I wish my daddy had trained me for the Ministry, but what's the use? Then across the river I seen the flicker of our campfire, an' heard the faint tinkle of the horse bells. I dunno why, but that seemed quite a help. I don't waste any time lookin' for a ford but hit the river just where I was figurin' I'd just as leaf drown as be dessected. I was shirt pockets deep a couple of times, an' this'n is a glacial river, but that evenin' I didn't know if it was freezin' or boilin'.

About two hundred yards from camp, I managed to let out a sort of croak, an the Pilgrim an' ol' Greasy hollered back. I sat down then to stop my knees from shakin' plumb out of their sockets, an' to let my hackles smooth down, an' generally catch up on my sang froid.

THAT NIGHT WE was loafin' around the campfire. I'd had a couple quarts of coffee, as well as the liver an' fixin's.

Life is lookin' some better than it did that mornin'. The blister ain't as bad as a broken laig, an' I figger a crack in a rifle stock ain't goin' to lose me no Trophies in future hunts.

Says the Pilgrim again: "Tex, I still say it's worth about five hundred Gold Standard dollars, just to be alive an' out in the hills."

I shuts my eyes hard a minute, an' right away I see that she-Grizzly on the trail behind me. When I open 'em again I says, real fervent-like, "Pilgrim, you tellin' *me?*"

National Sportsman, September 1936, 16–17

SEVENTEEN

Tex Takes a Trophy

Tex recounts a different kind of trophy hunt—one in which not the size of the ram's horns, but the difficulty and challenges of the hunt make up the pay-off. He takes care to point out at the beginning and at the end that he has no time for persnickety hobbyists who measure horns and antlers as a means of ranking trophies, and he is also careful to point out that he is hunting for meat as much as for any other reason. As in other places, a strong ethical sense about the proper use of an animal's flesh and thus about the ethics of hunting informs this piece. Carrying eighty pounds of meat and a large trophy head down a mountain and then all the way home is no mean feat—it's a classic example of virtuous mountain masculinity.

—AG

Tex Takes a Trophy

———————— • ————————

A Pipestone Letter
By N. Vernon-Wood

—WB Ranch
Pipestone Creek, Alberta

Mr. John Lincoln
Wall Street, N.Y.

DEAR FRIEND:

I got them dope sheets you sent me, so that I can measure heads in a scientific & academic manner. An' then what?

Somehow I can't get all spraddled out about weather Bill Goofus' Elk is $^1/_4$ inch bigger than Doctor Bohunkuses, or if the specific gravity of my Ram is specificer than yours.

What I do know is that I had me one hell of a time stalkin' my Ram. He was layin' down on a ledge about a million feet above the valley when I spotted him through the old eight-powers. He'd shure picked his roost with judgment & foresight. There was an onobstructed view in nineteen different directions, an' nothin' but alpine meadow an' slide rock on both sides & below. A Rock Rabbit couldn't have crossed within a half a mile an' kept under cover.

I'm huntin' alone that day for the dual purpose of providin' meat for family eatin' an' accumulatin' a head which I can tack to the cabin wall to look at durin' the long winter evenin's. This one looks like he'll answer both purposes, but they's a turrible lot of terra firma piled up on end between him an' the fambly skillet.

The only thing to do is circumnavigate that mountain he's picked for his meditations, an' climb over, comin' at him from behind an' above. So I picket old Baldy, tie my coat & other doodads onto the saddle, an' barge off afoot, with four-five shells, a handful of dry prunes, & a empty rucksack.

It's a axiom that the closer you are to the base of a mountain, the farther around it is.

I've got to keep to the timber until I've circled enough to get out of the Ram's line of vision, an' when I started off the day was right hot, an' the mosquitoes was makin' one last stand before the early frosts put the run on 'em.

The traveling wasn't any boulevard either, bein' mostly deadfall an' underbrush. It must'a took me two hours to get to where I could do an Excelsior, an' reach for higher & better things. It's another two gainin' altitude, an' I was perspirin' free an' copious. That ain't quite the word, either. I was sweatin' like a loco Bull.

I stopped in the lee of a big limestone rock to cool off, an' noticed that there was a big bank of black cloud comin' up from the east, an' that the wind had swung from the southwest, until it was right behind that storm, drivin' it along.

The thing to do is do it pronto, so I start to stalk down for the ledge an' the Ram. I ain't seen him as yet, but I've got a pretty good idea where that guy is. Not more than three hundred yards, I think, so I start right careful, so's not to start any rocks slidin' & racketin', stoppin' frequent to check over the terrain.

The wind held steady, blowin' across from my left, but it's gettin' a edge on it, an' instead of going round it cuts plumb through a man. Then I see the Ram. That is, I could see the back sweep of his horns, but nothin' else to make a target.

I'm in a spot. From where I'm crouched on a slab, they's nothin' but loose shale that'll rattle the minute I put a foot on it. I can't get any place by goin' down wind, because there is a gully that might be easy for the Everest expedition, but for a waddy without a rope or pitons, it's useless. So what? Wait him out, an' when as or if he gets up, slap him down agen, or scare him up, an' take a chance on plasterin' him while he's on his way?

Havin' toiled thus far, I decide to play poker, an' wait. I got into as comfortable a stance as the mountain allowed, an' reached for the makin's.

They're in my coat on the saddle, an' for purposes of consolation might as well be in a Scotchman's pocket in Auld Reekie. So I eat a prune. Did you ever eat a dry prune, when you whole system is cravin' about six drags of Bull Durham?

Then that squall snuck up on me. First it hailed, an' the wind drove the stones like BB shot. Then it snowed. Wet, juicy flakes as big as spuds, an' then it settled down to a nice steady rain. There was times I couldn't see five feet in any direction, an' I'm scared that Ovis will quit the country, an' me know nothin' about it. Just as the snow was quittin', I heard a click below on the shale, an' threw off the safety, just in time to see a shadowy form driftin' across the talus down wind. I let her flicker, an' he come down bang, an' then got up, goin' downhill on three legs and a swinger. He's hit bad, or he would've climbed, so I follow the blood trail, takin' care not to crowd him. He'll weaken an' lie down if I keep back an' let him take his time.

At that it's gettin' dusk before I locate him layin' in a gully, just above the grass lands. The next shot finished him, an' it was plumb dark when I'd finished skinnin' an' dessecting. I loaded about eighty pounds of meat in the rucksack, an' takin' the head in one hand, an' the Springfield in the other, stumbled along to where my faithful steed is waitin'.

Only he ain't. When I get to where I left him there's only a busted picket pin. An' the makins' are still on the saddle.

THE SKY WAS TURNIN' gray in the east when I finally dragged myself into the shack. The wife bawled hell out of me for lettin' that old knothead come home with an empty saddle. Claimed she was scared to death, although she shure didn't sound like a frightened woman to me.

I still got that head. Personal, I don't give three whoops in Sheol if you or anyone else has a bigger one. It's hangin' over the fireplace, an' every time I look at it, I forget how cold & miserable & smoke-hungry I was. All I know is that it was one of the best day's stalkin' I ever done. You can't put that in no record book.

I'm goin' to take a flock of dudes down to Lake Minnewanka next week for fishin'. It anythin' interestin' develops, I'll give you the low down.

Yours truly,

TEX.

Hunting and Fishing, October 1936, 7

EIGHTEEN

SAWBACK CLEANS A LAKER

Another Pipestone Letter, this piece pokes gentle fun at the outrageous yarns and antics of Tex's sidekick Sawback and at the credulity of the paying customers. It is straightforward in that it has no tension regarding Tex's usual issues: civilization vs. wilderness, masculinity, class, and gender.

Although this story is explicitly set at Lake Minnewanka, just outside Banff (Aylmer Point is mentioned twice), this story was clearly written to appeal to American readers: When the fishing is good on this lake, Tex writes, "all you got to do is heave over yore hook with a pants button or just a written invitation onto it, an the Lakers will grab on like a Congressman to a PWA appropriation." The Public Works Administration was a godsend to Depression-era communities and their congressmen. The image of elected officials eager for appropriations and ear-marks was as familiar then as it is now, apparently. This story illustrates clearly that while Tex did not disguise the Canadian Rockies, his stories were not about specific places or place, and were intended primarily for American readers.

—AG

SAWBACK CLEANS A LAKER

———————— • ————————

Another Pipestone Letter
By N. Vernon-Wood

WB Ranch
Pipestone Creek, Alberta

Mr. John Lincoln
Wall Street, N.Y.

DEAR FRIEND:

Me an' Sawback Smith just got through with a flock of Piscatorial Pilgrims that came up for the fall lake troutin', and they shure got all the breaks. Every so often a man can hit Lake Minnewanka when conditions are just right, so that all you got to do is heave over yore hook with a pant's button or just a written invitation onto it, an' the Lakers will grab on like a Congressman to a PWA appropriation.

Honest, I've et so much fish this last while that I have a hell of a time restrainin' myself from jumpin' at flies.

When we arrove at the scene of our fishin' picnic, things was looking some propitious. We pitched camp at Cranberry Bay, drug our home-made puddle duck outer the cache, an' Sawback paddled the fevered Pilgrims out while I stayed in camp to build a bannock. You don't get blisters on your mitts from cookin', less'n you get too clost to the fire.

There's one disadvantage about lettin' Sawback off alone with a flock of Pilgrims. As a recontoor he shure fancies hisself, an' is apt to take the bridle off his imagination an' turn it loose. Unless you're present, it's right embarrasin' at times to corroborate. A Pilgrim after he's had a tete-a-tete with the ol' prevaricator is liable to look at you, more in sorrer than in anger, an' say: "Why didn't you never tell me about the time you shot the Game Warden, Tex?" or: "What's this I hear 'bout you an' the debby tante? Let's hear yore side of it, you ol' hellion!"

Anyway, it's not long before I notice that Sawback and the Pilgrims have left the bay an' are off Aylmer Point, an' also that they are catchin' fish. Well, that's what we're here for, an' I'm at peace with the world. I get supper all fixed, except I don't cut any ham, figgerin' there'll be broiled Lake Trout for the piece of resistance. An' there is. When the fishermen come ashore they bring along a coupla eatin' Lakers, just right for broilin'.

One of the Pilgrims has brung a fish scale & tape along, an' insists on weighin'-in the catch, keepin' a record very scientific & business-like. He's all a-twitter to tabulate a series of statistics for future generations, showin' weight for girth & length, till fishin' ain't romantic any more. An' as he weighs & measures, my pardner takes 'em down to the edge of the drink an' cleans 'em, which should of made me suspicious. But as I say, I'm at peace with the world, an' wouldn't of suspected a cross-eyed hoss-thief of anything just then. So after vespers we turn in full of fresh fish and friendliness.

Next mornin's catch is good, an' the scientific Hombre gets quite a thrill when he gets a fish that's three pounds heavier than its size warrants. An' Sawback still insists on cleanin' & guttin' with little or no opposition.

'Longabout noon the wind kicks up the lake some, an' the Dudes look at the whitecaps with sudden respect. One of 'em speculates on how long a man would last, s'possin' he's upset 'way out in the middle. An' that brings up the question of how many lives the lake has claimed. The answer is none, to my knowledge, an' I'm just about to say so when Sawback turns his wolf loose. To hear him tell it, this stretch of water is the grave of forty Injuns, 25 prospectors, five–six Dudes, an' ontold Wapiti, Moose, & Pack-rats.

"An' they ain't found the last corpus delectable yet," he says. "Ol' Coyote Bob's canoe was found last week, down at the fur end, but they ain't been no sign of him to date."

Sawback pulls a long face an' looks real mournful, but my ears stand up. I seen Coyote only a coupla days ago, just before we left town, an' he looked pretty healthy to me. Coyote's about the orniest citizen in these hills an' mean as a blind Rattler, but the Lord don't seem ready to gather him in quite yet.

160

However, I don't spoil Sawback's yarn. If he wants to thrill the Dudes, it's all included in the price they're payin'. We don't charge extry for nothin'.

That evenin' the statistician records another extraordinary weight for a Laker he's caught, an' I sneak down on Sawback as he's cleanin' 'em. I watch him open the Trout, an' see it's loaded clean to the gills with sand & small stones.

"So you're helpin' along the cause of academic investigation, are yuh?" I ask.

He grins, plumb unembarrassed. "I'm just tryin' to keep ol' Scales & Notebook enthused," he says. This bein' all the same difference to me, I shrugs, an' lets him go on.

That evenin' he inviggles the Student to go out with him again. They head for Aylmer Point, an' at dusk they come in with a whoppin' big Laker. Sawback totes it into the light of the fire, an' after it's weighed an' entered, opens it up.

Suddenly he stops an' says, "Sumpin' funny about the feel of this'n."

The Dudes watch as he slits it. Sawback sinks his hand into the plumbin', an' when he pulls it out he's holdin' up a Ingersoll watch by the chain.

"Goddlemighty!" gasps Sawback, staggerin' back; *"Coyote Bob's!"*

He rubs the back clean, holds it up to the light, an' shure enough, scratched on the back is R.S., which are ol' Coyote's initials. Robert Short's his full monicker.

The statistician turns kinda green, an' his voice quavers. "How many Trout we caught off Aylmer Point?" he asks, kinda hollow-like.

"'Bout six or seven," answers Sawback, "that we kept for eatin'."

The Pilgrim turns to me. "'Tex,'" he says, "from now on it's bacon & ham, you hear? I ain't goin' to eat no more Lake Trout, no how—*never!*" With that he dives into the teepee an' don't come out the rest of the night.

Later, when we was in our own rag house, I says to Sawback, "Smitty, far be it from me to criticize yore teckneek, but the next time you find a deceased rannie's[1] watch in the trout's innerds, you ougtha see that it ain't tickin' an' the initials ain't your'n."

Which he said he would.

Yours,

TEX.

Hunting and Fishing, December 1936, 12

1. A guy, a guide.

NINETEEN

SAWBACK CHANGES HIS MIND

This story is one of a pair, written at some remove from each other, that addresses a trip with a long-time client, Doc Kent and, with his new wife, Diana (Di). In this version, Sawback is skeptical at first, but is won over, as is Tex, by the woman's "sporting" nature, good sense and ability to climb and hunt, reversing gender roles and winning the mountain mens' approval for her ability to assume mountain masculinity. Di insists on first names (and an abbreviation at that), carries her own rifle through the mountains, refuses to give up trailing a gut-shot animal until she finishes the job, and skins it herself (thus getting properly dirty, of course). She is, therefore, a proper hunter, and a "reg'lar," one of them: not just an honorary man, which would not yet be much, but an honorary mountain man. In the other, less charitable, version, "It's a Woman's World," the female client plays it closer to the gender conventions of the time, refuses to climb or participate in the strenuous business of stalking or skinning, preferring to stay near camp; but she manages cool-headedly to bag three prime specimens within walking distance of camp, while Tex and Doc scramble up and down mountainsides to no avail. Her aplomb and success as a hunter win her the guides' grudging respect. The Pipestone Letters, written in the middle of Tex's writing career (1932–37), are characterized by a high generosity of spirit; some of the other stories concentrate more on mischief, low fun, or cussedness. A photograph of Diana standing with a rifle and a felled mountain goat on scree completes the story.

—AG and JR

Sawback Changes His Mind

————————— • —————————

Another Pipestone Letter
By N. Vernon-Wood

WB Ranch
Pipestone Creek, Alberta

Mr. John Lincoln
Wall Street, New York City

Dear Friend:
I get a letter from Doc Kent last summer, which amongst other things says, "You don't have to put on any frills, Tex. She is a good sport, and wants to rough it just as I have done on previous hunts."

I shows it to Sawback, who remarks, "Mebbe yes, but I'll bet you that hand-made skinnin' knife agin fifteen centavos, that we add Ladies' maidin' to our other accomplishments before the trip's over."

We ain't either one of us feelin' so good about this, an' that's a fact. The Doc has been comin' west every fall for quite some time, an' we've got past the Guide and Pilgrim stage. We've smoked each other's tobacco, used the same towel, an' shivered ourselves warm on the same summits. Onetime, Sawback has stopped a grizzly that was hell-bent on takin' Doc apart, an' Doc has plumb ruined one vacation by quarryin' a busted appendix out of me. An' now he's been an' committed matrimony, we do speculate some on how a Park Ave. gal is going to fit into a teepee, an' if she'll pack her own rifle.

"It might be an idee for you to practice up on callin' them knot-headed

165

cayuses somethin' besides what you generally do," I tell Smitty. "Mebbe she won't appreciate your intimate details of their ancestory.

"You're tellin' me, eh?" he comes back. "How about you usin' a little gentlemanly restraint yourself next time that passel of equine orneryness you call a saddle-horse wampoos with you. Last time she dumped you off, even my sunburnt old ears fried."

So, feelin' like I'm the chief mourner, I take the buckboard down to the deepo when the time comes to gather up Doc an' his impedimentia.

He comes boilin' off the cars lookin' right fit for a guy that's been settin' in a office prescribin' for Dowagers. "Tex, you old hellion, you're appearin' just as young an' twice as ornery as ever; this is my wife."

"Glad to meet you, Mrs. Kent," I says, tryin' to like I meant it.

"The name is Diana," she comes back; "Di to you. I feel that we're friends already."

While me an' Sawback is saddlin' up the knotheads I tell him what she said, an' venture the opinion that she might be reg'lar, but that the time to make shure is after we've stalked a goat for about a million feet, to find that in the meantime he's gone places.

"Why wait for that," answers the old misogynist. "They ain't none of 'em reg'lar in camp. It's temptin' Providence, an' jeopardizin' a beautiful friendship, not to mention crampin' our style, to lug any female into the hills. Me, I'm agin it."

On the way to the huntin' country she kind of makes a hit with the old longhorn though, by not tryin' to be helpful. If they's anything that gets him onhappy it's havin' one of these-here willin' little helpers around camp, male or female, that insist on helpin' with the chores.

We are camped under The Monarch to the east of Wapoose Pass the first time I take Mrs.—Di huntin'. As per usual I aim to try her out on Goat, them same Oreamnos havin' been created special for guides to blood Tenderfeet on. They are plentiful, not too hard to stalk, but at the same time, frequentin' country that will give you a good workout gettin' up to them.

The first one we see is roostin' way up on a grass slide, without any cover within a million miles of shootin' distance, an' he knows it; so we pass him up, an' toil up a mess of broken rock, mighty steep, big enough to make poor footin', an' generally lousy. I made a jestchure of carryin' her gun, kind of feeble, I'll admit, but it don't have to be very convincin' for most females to take you up.

"I'll let you lug it sometime, Tex," she says, "when my arm's broke."

166

I'm beginnin' to like that woman, by Judas.

Long about two P.M. we get a poke at a pretty nice Billy. No, she don't lay him out with a well-aimed shot in the heart. She aimed there all right, but planted a 6.5 in the digestive arrangements.

We have to trail that fool Goat about six miles an' up to the top of several unnamed peaks before she lays him out. An' before she does it, we navigate some ledges that are right horrific, what with snow an' ice an' straight drops. I suggests once that we call it off; but, no sir, leavin' a wounded beast don't fit in with what she calls the Fitness of Things. When we finally stop that Goat, he drops about a hundred feet straight down. If they hasn't been a snowbank for him to land on, he'd sure be plumb ruined.

It's dark when we get to camp, but Sawback notices that her hands wouldn't make no advertizment for Front's Honey an' Almond.

"Did she help you skin that goat?" he asks.

"She did, an' what's more she took out the tenderloin with ease an' facility."

He comes as near smilin' as he ever does, an' carries a pail of warm water to where she is washin', an' as he goes I hear him mumble, like he don't quite believe it himself, "Red-Eyed Old Jiminey, she must be reg'lar."

Which she was.

Yours,

Tex.

Hunting and Fishing, April 1937, 9

TWENTY

TEX TANGLES WITH HORRIBILIS

Tex uses the coarse language of the times ("Chinaman," "Chink," and "coolie"). He is afraid that he has mistaken a Chinese worker for a bear and shot him by mistake. His tongue-in-cheek remarks are at best ambiguous: "Chinamen are sort of sacrosanct up here, a paternal govt figurin' they are plumb harmless, an' oncapable of protectin' themselves in the Crude West, so it costs a man plenty even if he only takes a playful poke at one. I figger that for blastin' one I'll get hung." It does not stretch charity to read this at face value as implying that Chinese workers were indeed harmless and that he was in fact afraid that he might just have shot someone who posed no threat. But the jocular tone is jarring even if it is meant to be of a piece with Tex's mountain persona. The racist language and tone make it hard to read this story with enjoyment today.

—AG

Tex Tangles With Horribilis

———————— • ————————

Another Pipestone Letter
By N. Vernon-Wood

—*WB Ranch*
Pipestone Creek, Alberta

Mr. John Lincoln
Wall Street, New York City

DEAR FRIEND:
There is quite a argument at the Post Office last time I'm in for my mail, if any.

Old Coyote Ben who traps the Pallisser is holdin' forth on Bears: their habits, dispositions, how hunted, an' the best way to render down their oil. With a few added remarks on the price of hides, an' how that the best Bear hunter in the Northwest Territories, Rupert's Land an' the Yukon, is ondoubtedly a old ranny called Coyote Ben.

He's holdin' forth plumb authorative on Grizzly, an' I have some difficulty gettin' old Cameron to quit listenin' long enough for him to riffle through the W, X, Y, an' Z pigeonhole to find out if there's been any Optomists who think they can sell me a saddle, or collect for the one they sold me last spring. I'm sortin' out the batch, tryin' to find something' that looks like it ain't a nasty letter from a creditor, when I hear Ben say:

"Scared of 'em? No sirree, I've hunted 'em goin' on thirty year, an' I ain't seen the Bear yet that could throw a scare into me."

Which same crack makes me think that while the old fictioneer might've

171

hunted 'em plenty, he'd caught up on mighty few. Me, I've monkeyed around the berry patches an' wild-onion beds, lookin' for Ursuses quite some too, an' I've been scared plumb to death more times than I can remember.

There's onetime I'm comin' down the Kananaskis with a Pilgrim who's out for Grizzly. Just as we come out of a jackpine grove to where the trail skirts a mess of broken rock from some old landslide, I spot a fair-to-middlin' Horribilis pokin' along towards us. I grab our pack pony, tie up the saddle stock, an' tell the Dude to get organized, an' when the Bear comes 'round the bend in the trail to let him have it. I ain't worried any; I've seen the Dude shoot, an' at a tomato can at a hundred yards he's bad medicine. When that Bear comes along, he won't be over seventy-five, an' right in the clear. It looks like a cinch. In just about two minutes he shows up, an' the Pilgrim takes a long careful sight. Bingo—an' the bear swaps ends so quick his hind feet get tangled up with his front ones an' he goes offen the trail over the edge into them rocks in half a split second.

"I got him, I got him!" hollers the Dude. "Bet I hit him plumb center."

I ain't so shure, so I have him chuck another shell into the barrell, an' we sneak up easy. I can't see any blood trail, an' I suggest that mebbe it was a miss. The Dude is some dudgeoned, an' insists that Bear is layin' in them rocks, dead as the Townsend Plan.

'All right, let's go find him, but be ready to shoot in case he ain't so dead as you think."

My rifle is in Calgary, gettin' a busted stock fixed an' I'd left the ranch with a .45 Colt. We ain't been searchin' them rocks two minutes when I notice the Pilgrim is behind me. I sort of ooze over, an' comin in back of him, seein' he has the rifle, an' started this thing anyway. It takes him about half a minute to circumnavigate me an' get in the rear agen, so we cover about ten acres of rockslide out-manooverin' each other in a circuitous manner. We're lookin' for Bear, but we're also spendin' considerable thought an' effort into gettin' the other feller in front. The Pilgrim is one up on me, when something' comes out of the rocks like the 20th Century comin' out of a tunnel. I hear the Dude's gun go off, an' I fall between a couple of boulders wonderin' if I'm clawed to pieces or just clean shot with a nice expandin' .30-06. No, it ain't the Bear. Just a damn Pa'tridge gettin' up, but the result on our system's synominous.

THERE USED TO BE a hotel way up on the mountain above Banff, an' they kept their meat an' air-tights in a sort of combination ice-house an' pantry, just outside the kitchen. Bein' built on a side hill, they's quarters for the

Chinese staff below. One spring a Black Bear discovered that all he had to do to make a fat livin', was pry off the odd board, an' reach for steak, chicken, jam an' sow-belly. He's raided the cache two–three times, when the woman who run the deadfall says she'll pay me ten dollars cash to ruin that bear, so I drifts up the hill one evenin'.

I have a light left on, in the kitchen so it shines through the window onto the meat-house, an' take a room upstairs overlookin' the onsemble. It's dark as the inside of a black pony at midnight, when I hear a board splinter. I peek out, an' shure enough, there's a black blob outlined agen the cache. I draw a bead and shoot twice, quick. Minglin' with the bellerin' of a wounded Bear, I hear the damdest Ki-Yi-Mukka-Hi-ing I ever heard in my life. Lovely Lizzie, I think, I've made a double, an' got a Chink as well as a Bear. I'm scared to go down an' look. Chinamen are sort of sacrosanct up here, a paternal govt figurin' they are plumb harmless, an' oncapable of protectin' themselves in the Crude West, so it costs a man plenty even if he only takes a playful poke at one. I figger that for blastin' one I'll get hung.

However, I sneak down to learn the worst. I find a dead Bear 'bout fifty yards from the kitchen, but no Chink. He shows up about noon next day. Seems like, findin' life dreary up the hill, he's been in town consortin' with the laundry coolie.

Just as I shoot the Bear, he arrives seekin' his virtuous couch, an' the Bear dashes by him bawlin' like hell. The Chink doesn't stop till he lands in the Police barracks back in town. It's a good thing for me that I have a dead bear to show the Sargeant next day, or I'd be workin' for nothin' yet. Anyway, don't let any of them Bull Artists tell you that you can hunt Bear, an' never feel the hair on the back of your neck tryin' to get up to the bald spot on top.

Sincerely,

Tex.

Hunting and Fishing, May 1937, 15 and 46

TWENTY-ONE

NAVIGATIN' FOR NAMAYCUSH

"Namaycush," the fish in this story, is an aboriginal word for fish, but the full term refers to the biological name for a type of freshwater salmon found in central and eastern North America, *Salvelinus namaycush*. It is possible that Tex could have known this aboriginal word, but since the word does not refer to fish or groups of Native people found in the Rockies, it could also be that Tex knew the scientific term. It is not the only time that Tex uses correct scientific terminology (see "Rams"). Instead of a way to showcase his work for the Smithsonian, this time the technical reference is the source of the joke in the story, where Tex pretends that he and Sawback have been conducting "scientific" research during a rather unfortunate attempt to catch a fish. As in other stories, Tex combines down-home phrases with Latin references, classical allusions, and Hollywood to make him seem as if he belongs in the Rockies, but can make fun of redneck habits at the same time.

—JR

Navigatin' for Namaycush

By N. Vernon-Wood

It's that time of year when winter dallies in the lap of spring, an' the geese are flyin' north. It's open season for bear, poets, an' sulphur an' molasses; time to oil saddles an' think about breakin' the odd colt. It's also the season when you're always sort of fed up with what you have been doin', an' get to wishin' you was a parson, or a fan dancer—or somethin'.

I've just got in from the Kootenay Flats with a bunch of ponies I'd wintered there, an' if you think I didn't have one hell of a time, you're crazy. Them bone-heads was feelin' altogether too good, an' I wore out three good saddle horses hazin' them critters hither an' yon. Just about the time I'd have 'em headed down the trail for home, some onredeemed filly would duck her nut, kick at the sun, an' tear off into the timber in the general direction of Vancouver, takin' half the herd with her.

By the time I'd have them headed off, the rest of the bunch would be loopin' down the back trail, like cats shot in the tail with a bootjack. However, I finally got 'em into the home pasture, after three days' honest-to-gosh bush wranglin', and am settin' out on the stoop, wishin' I was Clark Gable, an' that Jean Harlow was in the cabin makin' sour-dough biscuits, instead of me havin' to do it, when I hear footprints.

It's Sawback Smith ridin' his wall-eyed pinto. He drops the reins an' comes over. "Don't you never do nothin' but set an' lissen to the music of the spheers?" he asks.

"Shore; sometimes I set an' lissen to eegerious hombres that talk just to hear their teeth rattle," I tells him. "What's on yore mind, besides yore hair?"

177

"I figgered I could mebbe sell you a few bronks. I got more than I got range for, an' I'll make you a good deal on a flock of unbroke three-year-olds," he sez.

"You can't, an' you won't. I'm surfeeted with bronks, broke, unbroke, or just so-so. I don't give a long-drawn-out hoot in hell if I never see another horse, pony, cayuse, mustang, or even a three-toed eohippus. I'm goin' to shoot my own bunch, an' be a Vulga boatman, or a millionaire's chauffer. I'm fed up an' stove up, so you shut up an' unload that skinful of misery you're ridin', an' go inside an' rustle enough grub for both of us. When I've et, mebbee I'll feel more human. An' mebbee I won't, seein' who's doin' the cookin'."

As a matter of fack, Ol' Sawback is the best cook west of the Great Lakes, so about an hour later I'm feelin' more like a white man agen. I reckon that's what makes me strike at his bait.

We're layin' on the bunks smokin' when he asks: "Did you ever fish Devil's Lake this time of year?"

"Nor any other time," I tell him. "I ain't got a boat, it's too far off my range, an' what I don't know about lake trout would fill a liberry. Besides, there's good fishin' right here in the Pipestone."

"An' stream fishin' don't open till July, an' the lake will be legal on the 15th of May, which is four days from now. Jim Barker told me he'd loan me a boat any time, an' I can get Pat Rogers to drive us over in his flivver. Let's you an' me take a tent an' some grub, row down to the east end, an' camp for a few days. We can fish an' relax our souls; they won't be no ponies to wrangle, an' nothin' to do but angle an' eat."

It seems like a right pious idea. I shore need a change, an' settin' in a boat draggin' a spoon on the end of a line sounds right *dolce far niente*, as they say in Ensenada, so I lets myself in for it.

THREE–FOUR DAYS LATER, I hear what sounds like a chivaree comin' over a rough trail, an' Pat Rogers' chariot comes to a sudden stop with the radiator halfway through the gate.

Ol' Sawback unwinds hisself from the off gate-post, an' we load up our flea bags an' camping outfit. I take a rod an' reel along, in spite of Smitty's insistin' that they are onnecessary, this bein' a trollin' proposition.

Pat, besides bein' Irish, an' therefore some mercurical, drives like they's a warden after him, an' they's a couple times before we get to Barker's when I almost wish I was sittin' on some ornery knothead that is only just buckin'.

More by luck than judgment, we get to the lake an' find Jim's boat. We load our junk aboard, Sawback takes the oars, an' we push off.

There ain't any place where the lake is more than a mile wide, an' Sawback tells me that he saw 300 feet of a surveyor's chain let down before the end touched bottom, an' I don't need anyone to tell me that if the water was any colder, Sonja Heinie could use it better than us.

When the ice breaks up, which in this neck of the woods is around late April or early May, the prevailin' wind, comin' from the west gradually drives the ice down to the lower end of the lake. Here it piles up, makin' a field that sometimes you could drive a team over, an' sometimes not. Sawback claims that along the edge of this ice-pack is where the real top-hole fishin' is. Lakers runnin' up to 60 lbs., f.o.b. He says that as long as the water stays cold, an' the ice is there to make it colder if possible, the big fish feed close to the surface. As summer comes along, an' the temperature rises, then the trout duck for deeper depths, an' are fussy as to what they will strike on.

Well, the ice is waitin' for us. The last half mile of lake is plumb covered, so we beach the coracle, an' make camp about a hundred yards back in the spruce.

By evenin' we've got all organized, with a woodpile a jeraff couldn't see over. It seems kind of strange not to hear the horse bells, or worry about how far you'll have to walk for a saddle horse in the mornin'. Just before I drop off to sleep I say to Sawback that this looks like money from home. I've noticed that the grass here is belly deep to a tall Indian, which makes it a cinch that did we have the hosses along, they'd leave it an' drift eight miles to where it wouldn't run half a ton to the section. The only reply I get sounds like a dull buzz-saw hittin' a railroad spike.

Seein' Sawback's done the heavy work yesterday, I'm out first next A.M. an' start the coffee goin'. When the bacon is done, I stick my head in the tent an' ask can he stagger out an' get it, or does he expect room service. He grabs his pants an' a towel an' sprints to the lake, while I put one over by washin' in nice warm water in camp. I never was one of these-here cold-plunge addiks.

I hear Smitty makin' one godawful racket down to the lake, an' think mebbe I'd better drift down an' see has he dropped his store teeth in. When I get there he's cussin somethin' scandalous.

"That onmentionable dingey is adrift about 200 yards off shore, an' why in the name of the little pink pajamas of Frank Buck's pet python didn't you tie the perishin' thing up?" he wants to know.

"Shucks, I thought it was broke to stand with the reins down," I tell him.

WELL, WE CAN'T COAX it back into camp with a pan of oats, so we draw straws an' natchelly I get the short one. Nobody's ever complimented me on my figger; in fack, I got to stand twice in the same place before I throw a shader, so when I get cold, I'm cold all over an' plumb through. Before I've caught up with that gallopin' galleon I'm so chilled I'm spittin' hoar frost. I climb aboard, scrapin' enough hide off'n me to make a man-sized hankerchiff, an' paddle back to camp strokin' anyway 75.

Half an hour later, Sawback wants to know are we goin' fishin' or do I figger on standin' around camp all day, tryin' to shiver myself warm, so we go down to the oomiack, an' I haven't any good argument to bring forward when he says I'd better do the rowin' as the exercise will keep me from solidifyin'.

Did I say Devil's Lake wasn't any more than a mile wide? Mebbe it ain't the first three–four times you row across, but by the time curfew tolled the knell of partin' day somethin' has happened. That lake is not 10 miles wide, by 400 knots long. I've got a couple of half hitches in my vertibra, four blisters on my lunch hooks, an' a sliver where I can't see it. Sawback has enough trout to make a meal, if we use all four of 'em.

"What were you sayin' about sixty-pound trout?" I ask next morning, while I'm tryin' to straighten the kinks in my framework.

"They're here," he sez, "an' I know guys who have took 'em."

"Yeah, but you an' me ain't goin' to be any of 'em," I reply. "Me, I'm goin' to try this rod, with a spinner, an' play with the little fellers. You, Sawback, can come along an' play you're an outboard motor."

The lake is smooth as ten-year-old Scotch. Sawback pulls slowly along the edge of the ice field, an' I spot a rise just ahead. One of them slow, easy breaks, that generally indicate big fish. I've rigged myself with a six-foot leader, a No. 6 pearly spinner, with a slice of fish belly on for added attraction. The first cast draws a blank, but as I'm recoverin' on the second, I feel somethin' like I've snagged into a small log. There ain't any rush like a cutthroat makes, nor any of that vibration you get when you set your hook in a rainbow in swift water. I give a light pull, just to see am I into a sleeper or an old boot, an' that fish comes to life. He tries to get under the ice, an' I have a hell of a time turnin' him. Then he makes a run straight for the schooner, an' I'm reelin' in at 1100 r.p.m. as he ducks under the boat with a flock of slack line. Then he decides to go an' see if Sawback was lyin' about that 300 feet of chain, an' the rod looks like a barrel hoop. It's a good thing our pinnace is built like Kate Smith, because I'm bracin' my Number Twelves against the gunnel, an' Sawback is jumpin' around yellin' what he thinks is technical advice, but which I'm too busy to attend to.

Don't ask my how long that feller fought; you know dang well you'd lie about it yourself. But I have to wrangle with him quite a while. Of course, we don't have any landin' net, so I have to get him plumb tame before I reel him close enough for Sawback to slip his fingers under the gills and heave him aboard. No, he ain't any record in the light of day, but he'll go mebbe eight pounds, an' he's 128 ounces of hard fightin' meat.

"Lissen, feller," I sez, after I disgorge the spinner. "If these babies will come up for this, they'll rise to a fly. I'm going to try a Royal Coachman an' this Ibis that a pilgrim give me last summer."

"I always thought you was some loco, but now I know it. Nobody ever took trout in this man's lake except on a troll." This is all the encouragement I get, so I make a proposition. I'll fish off the ice pack, and Sawback can take the dingey an' drag his loors over the back, an' we won't be crampin' each other's style.

I CLIMB ONTO THE ICE, an' get ready to commence to begin. For a while it looks like the old hoss there is right. I cast, an' cast, an' cast some more, without a rise. I've got some fed up an' careless, when I see there's somethin' doin' at the boat. Smitty has dropped the oars, an' is hauling line. About twenty feet astern, a fish that looks like Moby Dick hisself busts water. An' just when I ain't attendin' to my own knittin', I get me a strike. I'm standin' on the edge of an ice pan that slopes down into the drink, like the gable end of a Dutch house, an' next think I know, I'm on the part of me that chairs are made for, slidin' slow but steady in the general direction of an unpremeditated bath. I cling to my rod with one hand, an' grab for a holt with the other, but on that ice there ain't any holts. Just as my pants begin to fill up, I roll over an' start to crawl real celerious. I just make it, but the tip of my rod's busted, an' ole Cristivomer is gone with my fancy Ibis an' half the leader.

"Gentle Joseph," sez Sawback that night for the ninety-seventh time, "but you shore looked superfluous, slippin' down that ice on your tail."

"Mebbe so," I reply, very dignified, "to a low mentality like yourn, but us pioneers always expect hardship an' discomfort when we're engaged in scientific research."

"Research?" sez old Sawback.

"Shore," I sez, edgin' for the portals of the rag house: "ain't I researched an' proved them namaycush'll take a fly?"

Which I figger I have.

National Sportsman, May 1937, 14–15

TWENTY-TWO

What's in a Name?

This late story (1938) echoes earlier satires poking fun at British hunters for their love of fancy equipment and gadgets, baths, shaving, and other civilian ablutions foreign to the proper mountain man in his mountain camp. The "pilgrim" disgraces himself both by his elaborate morning *toilette* and by making a noise that causes a prize moose to bolt. However, he redeems himself somewhat by shooting the moose later the same day, when it unaccountably shows up where the hunter and Tex are fishing. The sly introduction of a gentlemanly code of sportsmanship upends the dominant ethos of the piece—animal-savvy guides, stupid pilgrim—when the hunter shouts to spook the moose into running...

—AG

What's in a Name?

———— • ————

By N. Vernon-Wood

"Far be it from me," says Sawback Smith, "to cast any aspersions on your nationality, feller, but you gotta admit that huntin' with some of these here County families is what curdles the milk of human kindness, an' frays to hell the cinch that binds the Empire."

I'm taking the scalp off a ram, an' had got to the eyes, where you've got to use a certain amount of discretion an' a light hand, or you'll nicks the lids, so I just say Uh Uh, an' keep on skinnin'.

The Hon. Fitzwilliam Smyth-Smyth has plastered this Canadensis yesterday, an' seein' that his trophies has got to be shipped to some taxidermist in London who mounts 'em for His Majesty an' the Nobility, I'm tryin' to do a clean workmanlike job. There ain't gonna be no comeback about hair slippin' or sloppy fleshin', not if I can help it.

When I'd got past the eyes, an' was whittlin' down the nose cartilage, I ask Sawback what has stirred up the mud in the placid spring of his disposition this time.

"My old man come out here from Massachusetts before the Riel Rebellion, an' they's been Smiths in New England fur just as long as they've been in Slocum-in-the-Moors, Brummagemshire," says my side kick. "An' if that monocle-manipulatin' Gump-chinned woodbiner calls me a ghillie one more time, I'm a-goin' to re-enact Concord, Bunker Hill, an' Yorktown all over again on his desiccated frame."

"Shucks," I says, "it's a national habit. Ever since Bill Shakespeare asks,

What's in a name? the Cousin Jacks think they've got to be some casual. This one keeps a-callin' me McWhirter, an' you know that the only Scotch in me is taken from them dimpled crocks, as a antidote for incipient senile decay, an' to facilitate my justly famed rendition of Frankie and Johnny.

"I used to check him up at first, but he explains that the last hunt he made was in Muckle wee Stoor, an' his ghilly's name was McWhirter. Followin' that line of reason', by the time he's got around to huntin' Kudu he'll call some Swahili sourdough 'Tex,' an' what of it?"

"The last hunt I made," replies Sawback, "was with an Injun called Shaba Snooga, which is a name that embarrassed even Snooga hisself, an' it's a poor scheme that don't work two ways. From now on, I'm goin' to call the Hon. Fitzwillie, Snooga. Pity he don't savvy Stoney lingo, but just callin' him it will ease my feelin's some."

Which won't lead to no International complications, an' might help Sawback recover his armor proper, as they say in Boston.

Just the same, it does take a certain kind of Limey to get us bleedin' Colonials all puffy in the withers. This one has come out to accumulate a mess of trophies for his ancestral dugout, an' he's outfitted to the last details by Gamage of High Holborn. What with this an' that, our camp looks like a section of the Sportsman's Show, with Abercrombie trimmin's. First night in camp, Sawback got all embroiled with Fitz's special an' private tent. It's the Arctic-Safari model by the British Tent, Awning, Sail and Lorry Tarpaulin Mfg. Co. Ltd., an' as simple as the Fourth Dimension.

"Have you got the blue prints for pitchin' this jeesley shootin' box?" inquired Sawback, after the fifth attempt.

"Perfectly simple, my dear Bucksaw," replied Fitz. "You take this lanyard, pars it from the heah to theah, an' theah you are."

"An' then whereinhell are ya?" Smitty wants to know, just as the whole issue folds around his neck for the sixth time.

But it's Fitz' habit of miscallin' names, places, an' things that riles my buddy, who's one of these literal blokes, an' can't understand that the British mind works slowly its wonders to perform.

Anyway, I'd got that ram's scalp peeled, an' was rubbin' salt in the ears when the Pilgrim ambles over. "Jolly neat job of fleshing, what?" he gargles. "An' may I arsk what is on the agenda for tomorrow, McWhirter?"

"I ain't McWhirter," I tell him, 'but tomorrow I figger we'd best get an early start an' sneak up on a lick that's right popular with Moose. It's about three miles from camp, an' we can use saddle ponies most of the way. If we're skunked in the mornin' we can do a little fishin' an' try it agen just before dark."

"Right ho. I shall prepare the fishing tackle immediately, an' eliminate any unnecessary delay in the morning," says he, and he ducks for his perigrinatin' palace to sort out the correct impedimentia for a combined Moose stalk an' fishin' trip.

Sawback an' me roll out next A.M. long before sun shows up, an' while I rustle coffee an' hog's vest, he lights out to jingle the odd saddle pony. Just as the snow caps on the surroundin' peaks are turnin' pink, I heave a chunk of wood at the Honorable's balloon silk boodwar, an' yell "Come an' get your bloody wolf bait!"

It takes his lordship quite some time to wash, shave, manicure, an' tonic the hair, him havin' dispensed with the ministrations of his valet: said gent's gent havin' been left in Banff so Fitz can live the life of the raw, pioneer days, an' so on, what? He marches over to the fly under which I have spread the tools an' dishes, just as the tinkle of hoss bells tell me that Sawback is nearin' camp with the caballos.

"Greetin's an' salutations, McWhir—my man. But, tell me, why wolf bait? I thought we proposed to pursue the Moose today. Does one bait for wolves, really?"

"Merely a figger of our idiomatic speech," I tell him. "It's my uncouth way of announcin' that brekker is served in the mornin' room. You tie into the mush while I help Sawback catch a couple of plugs for ridin' purposes. This done, we join Fitz at the table, where he's deliberatin' between marmalade on mush, or bacon on marmalade, an' undoubtedly missin' his deviled kidneys an' kippers.

"Didja see anything while you was jinglin'?" I ask Sawback, meaning naturally did he see any fresh game, or fresh tracks.

"Yeah, I seen a Giant Panda half way up a spruce, an' they's been a couple of Okapis wallowin' in a mud hole up the trail a ways," he sez.

"Oh, come now, Sawhorse," says Fitz, "you're spoofin', what?"

"My mistake," renigs Smitty, "I mean a porcupine, an' a couple of moose calves. It's that book I was readin' last winter. It gets me sorta millin' around in my speech."

The Pilgrim is about as speedy as the Athabaska glacier when it comes to gettin' ready to start to commence to begin, but eventually he has loaded up, with rifle, binoculars, telescope, camera, fishin' tackle, spare cigarette holder, an' foldin' tin cup, so finally we're off.

A QUARTER MILE OR SO from the lick we tie up an' proceed afoot. We've got the wind, an' if they's a Moose on the lick we should get a shot, always providin' they don't hear Fitz whose numerous dinguses hung around an' about him, making him apt to rattle or jingle just at the wrong time.

An' that's just what happens. I'm trying to imitate a footsore Injun walkin' on eggs, an' could just see the withers an' antler tips of a bull through the timber, when Fitz hooked his camera strap in a dry spruce limb. It come loose with a crack like a .45-90, an' the Honorable Smyth-Smyth says "Oh blarst!" The bull says nothin', but makes a standin' jump of mebbe forty feet an' lights runnin'. For a couple of seconds we can hear him crashin' through the jack pine, an' the silence comes in large hunks.

"Beastly provokin'," says Fitz; "beastly. An' what do you suggest now?"

They're several things I'd *like* to suggest, but for the sake of universal peace, hands across the sea, an' all, I restrain myself.

"Let's go fishin'," is all I trust myself with, so we poke down to the creek in comparative silence.

Fitz shure can cast a nasty fly, an' for the next hour or so I sorta forget his failin's an' admire his teckneek with a tapered line an' his Bivisible. He's about forty yards downstream from where I settin' with his rifle and cetras, when I hear a sort of clinkin' noise, minglin' with the chatter of the crick. Lookin' upstream, I see a Moose crossin' over, with a head on him like you hear about an' seldom see.

I looked back at the Honorable, who is plumb intent on his castin' an' oblivious to me or the Moose. I don't do a thing to attract his attention, an' I wonder how soon that bull will get the flash of the Pilgrim's rod an' spook out of the country. Well, there's no use settin' like a bump on a log, so I grab the smoke pole an' start backin' downstream. Accordin' to the best authorities, that fool bull should've quit the vicinage forty different times before I got to where the Honorable is tyin' on a fresh cast. I'spect he thought I was gone loco at first, but he finally reads my signs, an' cool as the square-tail he's just landed, hands me his rod, an' reached for his fowlin' piece. He stands watchin' the bull, who's still fiddlin' about in the crick. Sometimes he's belly deep, an' again he's standin' up to his knees contemplatin' this an' that. I'm wonderin' why'n heck he don't shoot, when Fitz gives a shout. An' that's tore it all to hell, I think, as the bull makes a flyin' leap for the bank, but the rifle cracks once, an' old schnozzle puss folds up on the bank deader than fourteen Egyptian mummies.

Settin' by the campfire that evenin' full of liver an' onions, I'm tellin'

Sawback how Fitz busts the Moose. The Honorable is smokin' his Dunhill and cleanin' his rifle. "But what in hell did you holler at him for?" Sawback asks, some perplexed.

"Carn't shoot the bally things settin', you know. Besides, 'twould've been a jolly old chore if I'd dropped him in the watah, what?"

"Speakin' real personal," says Smitty, "I think you're just plastered all over with horseshoes."

"Really?" answers Fitz. "A combination of fortuitous circumstances, I should say, my dear Hacksaw."

Sawback spans the palms of our trophy for the umpteenth time. "Oh hell," he sighs, "you win. Call it any blasted thing you like."

Which he'd proberly do anyway, thinks I to myself.

National Sportsman, February 1938, 6–7 and 21

TWENTY-THREE

SAWBACK AND THE SPORTING PROPOSITION

Tex plays riffs all up and down the scale of language in this piece in a virtuoso register worthy of English satirist P.G. Wodehouse. The Indian fishing story trades on stereotypes about Aboriginal people as fascinating and yet uncultured, certainly, but it also gently lampoons the "sportsmanlike" fishing of the white protagonists with a slightly grudging nod to the efficiency and practicality of Aboriginal food-gathering. One senses here a form of reverse Romantic sensibility about the Noble Savage but this time the "Siawash" [aboriginal people], ironically called "noble aborigine[s],"[1] are the really sensible ones; while white fishermen insist on "sporting" conduct in an impractical way.

—*AG and JR*

---

1. See note 34 on page 27 for a discussion of the term "Siwash."

Sawback and

the Sporting Proposition

———————— • ————————

By N. Vernon-Wood

I'm CLEANING UP the winter's accumulation of empty cans, deer bones, an' other assorted detritus from around the cabin door, when Sawback Smith rides up.

"Beats all what a man finds when the snow gets to meltin', don't it Tex?" he grins. "You're lucky I ain't the Warden feller. Countin' them deer hocks an' hooves that're showin' up, I'd deduce that you shure overplayed your legal limit on venison durin' the winter."

As a matter of fack, them bones come out of only two deer, both of which was obtained as legal as my Pilgrims knowed how, an' Sawback knows it, and he knows that I know he knows it.

"Which only proves you've got a low suspicious nature," I reply. "Two thirds over half of them shanks an' hocks was drug over by my hound Herman from other an' adjoinin' stump ranches. That dog is quite a collector."

"He must be to freight a pile of bones that big, an' your nearest neighbor fourteen miles south. Lissen, d'you know what day it is, feller?"

"What's it matter?" I ask. "I know that winter's quit dallyin' in the lap of spring. I seen a pair of blue birds yesterday, an' there's a gaggle of geese on the west slough."

"Do tell! Well, there's also a fardel of fish down where Skookumchuck Crick empties into the lake. I dunno about you, but I'm fed up on lean venison, so I rid over to see if you'd consider postponin' your various

193

inutile pursuits, an' concentrate on decoyin' the odd Cristivomer outer his native element. Today's the 14th of May, you benighted old bullhead, an' lake fishin' opens tomorrow."

"Lightenin' Lucifer!" I exclaim. "I'd plumb lost track of the days. Wait'll I burn this heap of bones so's it won't cause any onmerited suspicion should the Warden blow by, an' I'll catch up my Goldie mare, an' be right with you."

Next mornin' we leave Sawback's dugout before dawn had even commenced to crack, and make the ten or so parasangs to the mouth of Skookumchuck in less'n three hours, which is right good goin' when you consider we got a pack pony loaded with various housekeepin' utensils, a tepee, an' a pair of 90 x 90 flea bags.

We pick out a camp spot, an' while I'm cuttin' a set of tepee poles, Sawback unpacks an' turns the cayuses out to graze. It don't take very long for two men who have hit the trails together for more years than either one will admit, to throw up a camp. We got the bough beds laid, the grub boxes set up on poles by the fire, an' a pile of dry jackpine split by the time the old Haymaker was well over the peak of Mt. Toby. Then Sawback starts draggin' a peculiar lookin' doohickus out of a canvas bag.

"Whatinhell you got there?" I ask.

"This," says the old misanthrope, "is modern man's answer to the need of a portable sampan. It's capable of transportation by pony, pack board, or under the seat of the family flivver. It's a newmatick boat, which when inflated draws two inches of water an' supports 600 pounds, weighs less'n a sleepin' bag, an' comes complete with a pair of paddles an' pump. I left the paddles to home, seein' we can whittle a pair with the ax, an' the pump is—blazes to blazes! Where is the pump?"

THIRTY–FORTY YEARS of amblin' up an' down our rugged frontier, consortin' with cow persons, prospectors, an' construction stiffs, have made me what you can safely call a connisoor of invective, recrimination, an' vulgar abuse, but listenin' to Sawback as he lay on his belly, blowin' into that rubber raft is a revelation. I wouldn't have believed any hundred-eighty pound hombre could find enough wind to blow into that craft, an' between whiles improvise such an avalanche of malediction an' imprecation. But he done it.

Sawback's feelin' sort of superfluous by the time he's got the wherry inflated, so I done the cabinet work, an' carved out a pair of paddles from a cedar. Even that don't please the old weasel. He claims I should've spelled him off on the puffin' act, but I explain that my boughten teeth made that some difficult an' besides, I'd never be able to think up the necessary objurgations.

So we boil water, an' after swillin' about a gallon of "guide" tea that would have slipped the hair off'n a brass monkey, we shove the caique into the drink, an' start to do what we come for.

I'm usin' a Colorado spinner, with a strip of meat, an' Sawback pins his faith on a medium size meat hook, tastefully decorated with a field mouse an' half a pound of lead.

"You got to go deep for 'em," he says. "Them lakers'll be down thirty-forty feet."

"In a pig's pocket they will," I argue. "It's plenty cold yet, an' you know dang well that they don't go down till it warms up."

"I know dang well they're down right now," Sawback says, his black hair bristlin'. "Lissen; I'll make you a sportin' proposition. If you kin catch a fish off'n the top of the water afore I kin from deep down I'll give you this blasted blow-up boat, free an' clear. But if you cain't, you gotta puff it full of yore hot air for the rest of this safari an' any an' all others we make together this season. Does that appeal to yore sportin' instincks?"

"It do," I says, quick as I can open my yap. "As the sayin' goes, yore hooked sucker!"

We're driftin' slowly down the lake, about 50 feet offshore. The water is still an' calm as a silver platter, except where a hell-diver is submergin' an' breaking out half a mile away. Not a rise in a hundred acres. Sawback lets out more line, an' I change to a Phantom minnow with lots of no success.

"You can say what you like," I tell Smitty, "But the Siawashes have the right system about this here lake fishin'."

"Which is what?" he asks. "Like lettin' the squaws do it?"

"No, like I seen 'em one time up the Cariboo. There's a stretch of drink called Long Lake, which shure describes it. It's 4 miles long, an' about 500 yards wide. The red brethren wait till it's froze enough to hold a horse, an' then pick out a narrer gut, 'bout half way up the lake. Then the squaws whittle out a few holes where they'll do the most good, an' set nets. Meantime the noble aborigine gathers a flock of cayuses, an' when the gals have done the manual labor, half a dozen bucks climb their war ponies an' hightail down the shore, drivin' a remuda of loose mustangs ahead. Then they fan out an' come down the lake like a cat shot in the tail with a skillet, an' the thunder of 30 or 40 set of hooves on that ice sounds like the drums of Tophet.

"Every trout in that vicinage spooks up the lake ahead of the ruckus, and lands in the nets. Then the damsels gut 'em and set 'em out to freeze. I seen a cord an' a half of fish piled in every wood-shed on the reservation."

Which Sawback doesn't believe, only it's true. I seen it done, though I didn't take no hand in sech unsportin' proceedin's myself.

BY LATE AFTERNOON we've drifted about four miles with no luck a tall, so we decide to paddle back an' take on a little nourishment, which we did. An' after loadin' up on lean venison, we sort of sit around smokin', watchin' the lake. As a successful fishing trip, it's a mighty good sit downer.

"Mebbe the thus an' sos will start feedin' about sundown," I suggest.

"They might at that," says Smitty. "What say we leave it lay until around seven o'clock, an' then give 'em another whirl?"

We carry the lung developer up to camp, an' loaf around the blazin' fire. Pretty soon Sawback begins to snore, an' I climb onto my hind legs an' prowl, to keep from makin' it a duet. Along about dusk, I heard a "plop" out in the water, an' I snooker down to investigate without wakin' the sleepin' beauty.

Lightnin' fishhooks, but they's forty-'leven rises in sight in one look! I injun back to camp, hopin' to slip one over on the sleepin' beauty. He looks the picture of masterly inactivity, so I sneak the paddle an' tackle down to the shore, an' come back for the coracle.

In a couple of minutes I'm swallowed up in the gloom, makin' wide casts with a burnished copper spinner an' a triple hook. I'm recoverin' about the third cast, when somethin' hits. Waitin' a second, I set with a flip of my rod rip. Whee-ee! goes the reel, an' Namaycush heads across the lake. When I've got him stopped, an' am crankin' to beat the band, I sort of notice that the pneumatic punt ain't feelin' just so, but I'm busy with what feels like a saw-log with a gift for divin'. There's a couple of right sizeable splashes alongside, an' I can just see enough to slip a hand under a gill, an' jerk my unwillin' passenger topside. He's a fish in any man's language, an' I bust him between the eyes to discourse his floppin' around, decidin' at the same time to paddle in an' wake up Smitty. I've won this aerated ark, so I might as well let the old billygoat know that from now on he goes yachtin' as my guest.

Seems like the craft don't surge ahead like it should ought to, an' I see that it ain't as bloated as it might be, so I put my back into paddlin'. I'm just sailin' into the circle of light from the campfire, when that danged dugout heaves a languid sigh, an' folds up under me. I'm settin' in three feet of turrible cold water, with a dead trout tryin' to float into the front of my shirt, an' listenin' to raucous an' vulgar bubblin' from the bank.

After I'm half dried out, I says, "Well, I got the first fish anyway, so I guess I'll put my brand on that dang boat after we salvage it in the mornin'."

"Hell, I can't see no fish," says Sawback, "an' if you ask me, your low unsportin' intrigue of leavin' me sleepin' while you snuk off, makes all bets off."

Next day I rescue the submerged shallop, an' checkin' it over, I notice that the valve is loosened just enough to cause a slow leak. I don't give Sawback the satisfaction of accusin' him of malfeasance, but I'm wonderin' if he WAS asleep while I was takin' my tackle an' the paddle down to the lake.

Some guys'll do anythin' just to win a lousy bet.

National Sportsman, May 1938, 14 and 26

TWENTY-FOUR

The Wild Goose Chase

The only story in this collection not signed "N. Vernon-Wood," this is also
the only piece not set in the Rockies or adjacent ranges (Selkirks, Cariboos,
etc). One reason for using a fictitious name is that another story of his,
"It's a Woman's World," appeared in the same issue of the magazine. Tex
seems to have been trying his hand at a genre piece outside of his own
immediate experience—or perhaps he hunted in New Jersey when visiting
one of his Wall Street or other New York clients [his daughter Dorothy,
herself also a mountain guide, on and off, until her seventies, visited
some of them in the 1950s, with my father Harry in tow—AG]. The style
is clearly the same as in the other "straight stories," and the gentle irony
alone would mark this as one of Tex's. It is worth noting that mountain
masculinity is transposed here into the register of winter masculinity; a
man's ability to withstand the cold functioning as a gauge of his hunting
prowess on cold marches and sea-shores in early winter. Success comes
only at the expense of considerable discomfort and risk, though these are
clearly secondary to the successful hunt and occasion some grumbling on
the part of the narrator.

—AG

THE WILD GOOSE CHASE

———————————— • ————————————

Hank the Viking puts out to sea in pursuit of a wounded gander
by Ramon Chesson
Illustrations by the Author

YOU'VE SEEN THE MARSH tossed and flattened by a cold, driving wind. You know how low, gray clouds sweeping in from the northwest can drive snow down your neck and chill you to the marrow. It's bad enough in daylight, but only a duck hunter can stand it before dawn. And only a most hardy duck hunter really likes it.

Hank is that kind of duck hunter. He has hunted ducks all the way from the east coast to the west. He has knocked birds down in the Louisiana bayous when you could fry an egg on a tin roof. He has lolled in the Texas marshes with his collar open and his sleeves rolled to the elbow and played pinochle between shots. But he'd rather get one duck in the south Jersey lowlands with a blizzard howling around his ears than to bring down ten with perspiration soaking his arm pits.

I guess I kind of like it, too. That's why we were both out there that morning. But even if you like a thing it can be overdone . . . or so it seemed to me after about an hour. The east had lightened almost imperceptibly. I hauled out my watch and leaned over to get the glow of Hank's cigarette on the dial. "Still plenty of time to wait," I announced. Hank got up, shook off the snow, and looked out at the white marsh. Then he settled back in the flimsy blind and puffed away. For stoicism, Epictetus was a bush leaguer.

After a while the east was distinctly gray. Hank got up, shook off the

201

snow, and looked out at the white marsh. Then he settled back in his corner, lighted another cigarette and declared, "This is the life!" I was silent.

"This is the best spot, you know," he said after a few puffs. I was still silent.

"Maybe we did get here a little early," he continued after a pause.

"That sounds reasonable," I agreed.

"But then," Hank observed, "we had to come early to make sure nobody would beat us to it."

I didn't remember seeing anybody groping around in the marsh looking for the blind. I still think we might have gone out there a little later without danger of finding the place occupied. However, there we were and there we stayed. And along about the time the sun must have been coming up somewhere back of that storm, we saw our first ducks. Funny how the sight of a flock of mallards can chase the cold away. The snow still drove through the gray pall of dawn. The cutting wind still whistled through our blind. Out across the bay the waves still whipped along with icy white caps. But when that old drake led his harem by a scant hundred yards to our left I actually broke out in a sweat. On they went. The few battered decoys we had thrown out in the dark might as well have been home in the shed. We stood straining our eyes as those ducks rode the tail wind out over the bay and were swallowed by the snow.

Hank pulled out another cigarette and squatted out of the wind to light it. Then he settled back in his corner. "You better stand up a while and watch," he suggested. "I'll sit back here and try to think of something."

I STOOD UP AND WATCHED. All I could see was a silvery gray expanse of flattened marsh, and I could only see a couple of hundred yards of that. Snow flakes as big as acorns were hurrying by on all sides. Our skiff was completely covered and looked like a muskrat mound. And my ears were frozen. Before long the biting wind seem to whisper in them that I was getting a raw deal.

"Listen," I said, crouching beside Hank, "I don't know what you're trying to think of, but I'll be glad to help you." So I bummed one of his smokes and we just sat there.

After about fifteen minutes the deadened report of a shot rolled by with the storm. From somewhere over the marsh came another shot. At last the inland duck hunters, the pond shooters, were getting busy. And that's where we came in, for we were on a point that afforded practically all the shelter the bay had to offer to ducks driven out of the ponds, and now that the war had started we forgot the cold and felt very happy about the whole thing. In fact, as well as I can remember, we were standing there in the storm exchanging congratulatory hand shakes when that first teal came by and brushed the snow off our caps. The little fellow made a short swing and plopped right in the middle of the decoys. We peeped over the top of the blind at him like a couple of G-men savoring the predicament of a cornered public enemy. And he saw us, too, for he sailed straight up into the wind like a kite. It was a beautiful shot. I still don't see how we both missed him.

The pond shooters were raising the devil by that time. Muffled booms were coming with regularity. And occasionally small bunches of mallards, black ducks and teal were coming, too. But there weren't coming close enough. All we could do was crouch there and cuss and pray and hope. But they still didn't come close enough.

"Maybe the decoys have blown away," Hank suggested. So we raised up on the other side of the blind to take inventory, and when we did about eight mallards came out of that bunch of decoys and started climbing. I won't try to guess how long they had been there. They went straight up in the wind for about ten feet and they looked as large as box cars. I heard Hank squall, "MEAT ON THE TABLE!" and we went into action. When that flock got straightened out we had three down. They were in close to shore with little chance of the wind taking them away, so we just let them lay and gave our attention to the marsh again.

"I can't understand it," Hank said after a few more flocks went by out of range. "They must be transients. They don't know the lay of the land or they certainly wouldn't pass up this cozy spot."

"Those last two words," I grunted, knocking the snow loose and pulling my collar up around my paralyzed ears. "Please repeat those last two words."

"Cozy spot," Hank blinked the snow flakes from his eyelashes. "Why?"

"Never mind," I said. "I'm in no condition to get into an argument. I was just curious." And I clamped my chattering teeth together and stared at a dark spot I had glimpsed swinging toward us through the storm. It was so low I thought at first it must be a man. And before I had time to warn Hank it was on us—a flock of a dozen geese flying so low they almost brushed the marsh! Before I could raise my gun they were passing, some thirty feet to the right. Now, Hank had picked that particular time to stand in the middle of the blind and gaze at the bay. To him, the first indication that something was happening came when I flounced around and upended both of us on the lee side of the blind. That flimsy construction wasn't erected to withstand a double assault, and it promptly collapsed. Hank had seen the geese, though, and amid the tangled rushes and general wreckage we proceeded to lay down what we hoped would be a withering fire, and despite the small size of our shot and the distance the geese had traveled during the confusion, it did look as if we had withered one old gander. The last one in the bunch began to lose speed and altitude, and just before the storm blotted him out he was flopping along only a few inches above the whitecaps.

We scrambled up and stood five or six minutes straining our eyes through the wall of snow, but it seemed the storm had conspired with that old goose and blew in harder than ever, hiding everything beyond a hundred and fifty yards of our wrecked blind.

Just then a bunch of black ducks sailed by and we both clicked on empty shells. After a series of concerted "damns" we reloaded and examined the bay again. "Well," Hank finally said, "we've got to get that gander."

I looked at him in amazement. "Hank," I spoke as quietly as I could, "once that skiff gets beyond the protection of the marsh it'll blow clear over to the Delaware side!"

"No," Hank was thoughtful, "the water is shallow out there. A boat can be poled through it. I don't believe it will blow away." He thought the problem over a couple of minutes. "I don't believe it will," he repeated.

"Well," I said, "I know how it is. A goose is a rare thing in this section and you hate to lose him. And since it's your idea, I think you're the man to get the gander."

We dug the boat out of the snow and while I stood by to yell and shoot, and generally act as a fog-horn in case he should lose sight of the shore, Hank the Viking put out to sea.

About two hundred yards out he turned at right angles with the shore and started poling along with more enthusiasm than progress. Between flurries of snow, I was able to follow his progress, and it was evident a race was going on out there. It was also evident that Hank was running a very poor second, for he suddenly threw the pole in the boat and began shooting. That's one way to win a race...or so you'd think. However, after two or three minutes he finally put the gun down, poled a few yards through the whitecaps, and picked up his victim.

Fifteen minutes later he was back on shore.

"That gander must have been doing a rare piece of maneuvering." I greeted him. "You did a durn fine job of shooting up the bay!"

"Now listen," Hank snorted between chattering teeth, "don't stretch my temper. Every time that cussed boat went up the gander went down. An now I'm going home. I got the goose and ducks. You get the decoys. The wind still cut like a knife and my ears were still frozen, but somehow, after seeing Hank out there chasing that goose, I didn't feel like I was getting such a raw deal after all.

National Sportsman, October 1938, 10–11

TWENTY-FIVE

IT'S A WOMAN'S WORLD

In this story, women get Tex's respect when they attain a type of "mountain manhood. " But in this case, mountain manliness is mediated by the domesticity of the heroine: she stays close to camp and avoids strenuous scrambling yet bags the most game. See a similar attitude about women in the remarks about the parallel piece, "Sawback Changes His Mind." In this piece, Tex's rustic sidekick Sawback expresses typical misogynist attitudes; Tex chides him for them but in doing so, uses a racist slur about Indian drunkenness ("we've guided many a female that took to huntin' like an Indian takes to lemon extract"). The female protagonist attains a variety of mountain manhood, but mediated, in this case, through the feminine gender role of domesticity. The moral here is rather different from those stories in which women accede to full mountain masculinity, such as the alternative version of this story (as above) or "This Guiding Business," but the message is still clearly that women can hunt and be mountain women, in this case.

—AG and JR

It's a Woman's World

———————— • ————————

Nello Vernon-Wood

"WHILE I'VE GOT NOTHING personal agin matrimony," says Sawback Smith, "I claim it should be confined to them areas sanctified by precedent and custom, like Niagara Falls, Bermuda, an' such. A huntin' trip's no place for the mele de lune."

"Mile of what?" I ask, mystified.

"That's what the pea soupers down in Quebec call the honeymoon," elucidates Smitty. "Only in this case it means miles of grief. Miles and miles of it."

"Ain't you squealin' afore the loop tightens?" I inquire. "I figger that if Doc is bringin' his bride along she'll probably fit like an old glove. He likes his huntin' trips too much to risk gummin' the works with a female he's only married to. I bet Doc's picked him out a gal what can take it, an' you know good an' well that we've guided many a female that took to huntin' like an Indian takes to lemon extract."

"Yeah," admits Sawback, "which is all the more reason why I'm spooky as a doe with fawns about this trip. Considerin' the law of averages, attraction of opposites, an' the axiom that woman's place is behind a bridge table, I got a forty-calibre hunch that we're in for bushels of trouble."

Well, we'll know all about it P.D.Q. Doc an' his newly acquired Missus'll

Reprinted in *Tales from the Canadian Rockies*, ed. Brian Patton (Edmonton: Hurtig Publishers, 1984; reprint Toronto: McClelland and Stewart, 1993), 248–252, by permission of William Vernon-Wood.

be in on the Trans Canada tomorrow, an' we are due to drag our tails for the East Kootenay the day after.

I'm down at the deepo with the rest of the hoi polloi next afternoon an' soon's the cars stop, I see Doc eruptin' from a Pullman accompanied by the followin': 1 woman, blonde, 1938 model; 2 rifles, Springfield, .30-06; 3 suitcases, 4 duffel bags, 5 novels, 6 cushions, an' 7 baggage checks to cover the rest of the impedimenta.

Other years, Doc comes boilin' out of the cars, an' grabbin' my hands says, "Tex, you blankety-blank onregenerate son of a blank-blank female coyote, how in blank are you?" an' I reply "Smile when you call me that, you dash-dash unprincipled appendix snatcher! Fine; finer'n frog wool!"

This time we're not so free an' unrestrained in our greetin's. I've got a idee that from now on me an' Doc have got to do our friendly cussin' only at such times as we're removed from the ennoblin' influence of lovely woman.

The two–three days it takes to get into the game country ain't what you'd call eventful, outside of the restraint Mrs. Doc's presence puts on Sawback's pack horse drivin' rhetoric. Them cayuses are used to bein' hollered at in man's language, an' to hear Sawback tryin' to keep them strung out on the trail without enlargin' on their ancestry, personal appearance, an' probable hereafter, struck me as right funny.

We get into camp at the head of the Horse Thief, and from where we've pitched the rag houses we can see a couple of goat sunnin' themselves on a ledge, only about a mile an' a half across, an' mebbe a thousand feet up. I check 'em over through the field glasses, an' decide they're billies, an' trophies.

All we got to do is sneak along the summit grasslands in the stream bed until we get behind an old moraine. From there I figger we can climb above 'em to not more than 150 yards away. It looks like an easy stalk. I'm explainin' this to Doc when his squaw asks do we ride, or go afoot.

"We go afoot, of course," I tell her. "In the first place, it'll take an hour to wrangle an' saddle the ponies, besides which we have to keep out of sight while crossin' this open country. After that, there ain't a cayuse in Canada could climb in that broken rock."

"I don't think I have the inclination to go scrambling about in all that horrible rock," she decides. "Haven't you got any goat somewhere down where it's all grass, and I can chase them on my pony?"

I let Doc explain the habits, disposition, an' method of huntin' billy goats to her, but I can see that she thinks it's all mostly hooey, an' that there must be better ways of bustin' a goat than to go side hill gougin' after 'em on your own feet.

"How far will this gun of mine shoot?" is her next question. "It would kill a man at 2000 yards, I suppose," replies Doc. "Well, why don't we walk along until we are below them? It can't be more than half a mile from the grass to where they are. If this gun shoots 2000 yards, I'm sure it should get one of those things at 880."

"Which it undoubtedly should," I chips in, "but it's got to have a heap of co-operation from the butt end."

Her only reply is a look that reminds me of the time I got caught by a blizzard while crossin' the Columbia ice field.

However, we get her started, an' injun along the crick bed until we get to where the goat can't see us, an' stop for a couple of minutes at the foot of a mess of glacial deritus an' slide rock. I point out a big old boulder just under a cliff, an' opine that if we climb to it, we'll be high enough to start a traverse that will bring us over our quarry, at the same time givin' us the wind on 'em.

Mrs. Doc takes one look, an' right there decides that she ain't lost any goat on that mountain.

"You men go ahead," she says, "and I'll stay here until you come back, or I get bored." I can see Doc waverin', an' before he can pull a bridegroom act, an' decide to stay an' keep her company, I start climbin' an' tell Doc to get goin'.

It's steep, an' broken all the way to the big rock, an' we're blowin' hard by the time we reach it. Stoppin' to catch our wind, I notice that the bride ain't where we left her, but I don't say anything to Doc, figgerin' she's probably settin' behind a scrub balsam or somethin'.

The traverse ain't so awful bad. Once across the moraine, there's grass ledges an' shale slopes, so we make good time to where I figger we should begin to start down. We sneak along, right circumspect, expectin' to spot them billies any old time now. After a while I whisper to Doc that I'd swear we're on the same ledge that we saw 'em on, so let's drift up wind a mite. That brings no luck, so we continue to descend, checkin' over every foot of the visible terrain.

Fifteen or so minutes later, we both stop with a jerk, as a shot rings out, an' echoes all over hell's half acre. Then another, an' whammy-bang-bingo; it begins to sound like a busy day in Madrid.

There's no sense stayin' where we are after all that ruckus, so we hightail down as fast as the broken country will let us. Doc is quite some trepidated, as he thinks mebbe the little woman has tangled with a grizzly, or seen a mouse or somethin'.

We found her settin' on a knoll about five hundred yards from where we left her, an' as Doc dashes up to see if she is still all in one bundle, she says, "You'll find your goat just over there, by the creek. I knew all the time it was just silly to go scrambling after them all over that mountain. I just waited until they came down to eat, and shot the biggest."

She had him, all right, but whoinhell would have expected them ornery critters to come down? An' the worst of it is, Doc goes all mushy, an' tells her that she's the best little hunter in five Provinces, includin' Rupert's Land an' the Arctic, 'stead of explainin' that she's lucky enough to fall into a garbage scow an' come out with a diamond ring.

Next mornin' Doc an' me take a pack pony over to the kill, and skin out the head, also savin' the meat for eatin' purposes. The little woman is left in camp, not being interested in the bloody details of side hill surgery. When we get back to camp, she's missin' and Doc has another spell of inquietude until she comes strollin' in.

"Oh, you're all here," she says. "Tex, do you suppose there is anyone else camped near here?"

"I don't reckon so, why?"

"Those are our horses up there on the slide, aren't they?"

"Sure, they're all there, except these three me an' Doc just got in with."

"Well, then," she says, "it's all right. That must have been a bear I shot down there on that grassy slope. I didn't go right up to it, after it fell down, because I didn't have any more ammunition, but I'm sure you will find it dead. I aimed right where its heart ought to be."

Doc an' I rode down to the grass slope, an' sure enough, there's a darn good black bear stretched out dead as Dan'l Boone. An' if you'd a' heard Doc gush all over Mrs. Doc that night, your stummick would have turned almost inside out.

After we've got the hides fleshed an' salted, we move camp down the valley a ways to harry the old wapiti. The elk are about, and every so often we hear the buglin' of some pugnacious bull, answered by another from across the valley. It's mighty sweet music, an' I figger on the Doc stoppin' a royal head before many days, an' as he's never accumulated an elk, we're both right up on the front end of our feet.

212

For three days steady we hunt the slides, with all the pediculous luck in the world. Any bulls we see are spikes, or measly little four-pointers at most. Or if we do see a real head, he's surrounded by a flock of jittery cows that spook for no good reason at all, takin' their lord an' master with 'em.

An' every evenin' when we drag our creakin' bones into camp, the little woman tells us about some "perfectly enormous" bull she's seen through the glasses right above camp, or some place where we ain't been. She's spendin' the days trying to get Sawback to try her recipes for crapes susies, an' marshmeller fudge, 'stead of good goat mulligan an' beans, but up to now, thank God, that old misogynist is stubborn, so we continue to get man's grub.

As we're leavin' camp on the fourth mornin' I tell Doc that if we see a ten-pointer, he'd best accumulate it. I've just about given up hope of gettin' a Royal, an' he agrees.

We eat our cold liver an' bannock that noon, 'way up on a hogback that separates two slides, an' there are eight elk in plain sight—four cows, two yearlin's, a spike buck, an' a scrub four-pointer. Across from the other side, another is buglin' and tellin' the world that he's the toughest guy of the whole Rockies, an' who'd like to make something of it? If we only had a trophy stretched out, it would have been the middle of a perfect day.

"Did you hear a shot?" asks Doc.

"Nope, not me," I reply. As a matter of fack, I've been half asleep. "Just a rock fallin', I expect. Come on, let's cross the valley an' see if mebbe that feller that's doin' all the blowin' is as good as he thinks he is."

It's a long way down, an' twice as long up on the other side, an' by the time we're out of the timber, that elk has quit advertisin' himself, so we still hunt until it's too dark to see our front sights.

Sawback has a big ole campfire goin', and settin' in its light is busy takin' the scalp offen a twelve pointer, with a beam durn near as thick as my leg. "Perigrinatin' porcupines! where'd you get it?" I ejaculate.

"Didn't," says he, "Mrs. Doc blasted him this afternoon. She went down to get a pail of water, an' this bird was standin' in her way, so she got her bang stick, an' banged."

"You know, dear," she says to Doc, as we're surroundin' a mess of stew," I think you shouldn't go tearing allover the country like you do. It's all right for the guides; I think they actually like it, but I'm sure my way of huntin' is nicer. Besides, look at the game I've got."

Her goat head is hangin' in a spruce, an' her bear robe is stretched on a frame by the tent. The elk is takin' up all the room in camp. I look, an' says to Sawback, "Hell, you just can't win."

He wags his head real doleful. "Tex," he says, "it's a woman's world."

Which now I figger it is.

National Sportsman, October 1938, 13 and 26

APPENDIX A

TEX VERNON-WOOD

———————— • ————————

Recollections by his grandson, John R. Gow

BACK TO THE FARM

AFTER HIS WIFE JOAN's death in the early 1960s, Tex went east to live with his son Bill and daughter- in-law Choukie [Christina], who were stationed at Trenton, Ontario with the RCAF. Both father and son remained keen outdoors people, often making fishing trips into the hills north of Trenton and Kingston, around the headwaters of the Mississippi River.

On one such trip, they were driving along a concession road through Ontario farmland, when Tex suddenly said, "Take the next road to the right." Bill complied, and made a few more turns as directed. No explanation for this route was given, until Tex directed, "Stop here!" They were at the turnoff to a typical Ontario farm. A lane ran a hundred yards up to a brick house; behind was an unpainted barn, all surrounded by tilled fields. A man, probably in his early seventies, was working in a nearby field.

"This is the farm I worked at when I first arrived in Canada," Tex said, "and it looks pretty much the same."

Tex went on to recount how, as a callow English youth, perhaps eighteen years of age, he had left England for good, looking for opportunity and freedom in Canada. His first job, lasting for the best part of a year, was on this farm in Ontario.

Source: Bill Vernon-Wood

As the only hired hand on a farm at the turn of the century, young Nello Vernon-Wood was treated pretty much as a member of the family. He lived in the same house, ate at the same table. The farmer and his wife had three children, two daughters and a son. The boy, youngest in the family, was about ten.

Along with his farm work, one of Nello's duties was to harness up the shay and take the lady of the house and the three children into church each Sunday. No record exists as to whether he himself graced a pew; a dubious proposition. At any rate, without the distractions of radio, television, and beyond, he came to know the family well.

Bill and Tex parked the car, and they walked up the lane. The farmer made his way over and greeted them.

Tex looked at this farmer, perhaps a decade younger than himself, and said, "I'll bet you don't remember me. The farmer took a hard look and said, "Not yet, but keep talking and I will." The conversation carried on, mostly about the possibilities of fishing in the area, but not a hint of the past.

The conversation carried on for five minutes or so, when the farmer suddenly interjected, "You're the Englishman who worked here back when I was a boy. When was that? Ought two, ought three?" There was little doubt in this farmer's mind as to whom he was speaking, in spite of a gulf of sixty years.

"I am indeed," Tex replied, " and it was ought three."

Bill and Tex were invited up to the house. Both sisters, now widows with grown families, had returned to live out their years with their bachelor brother on the family farm, both remembering Tex warmly.

Whiskey and Venison

At some time in the Twenties, Tex was on a pack trip up Simpson Pass, west of Banff near the present day Sunshine Village. Any hunting to be done would have to be on the British Columbia side of the pass, but the best camping was beside a small alpine lake, just on the Alberta side, in Banff National Park. Within the Park of course, hunting was strictly off limits.

The main quarry, Bighorn Sheep, were usually found on the shoulder of the Monarch, an imposing mountain just west of the pass, but were now proving elusive. The dudes were restless; the camp low on meat.

Riding back into camp one afternoon, Tex spotted a buck deer across a clearing, no further invitation needed. The fact that they were some yards east of A.O. Wheeler's newly installed concrete monument, which marked at once the Continental Divide, the Provincial border, and the Park boundary, was a trivial detail to hungry men. After all, a few minutes ago, the same deer was probably a hundred yards to the west and fair game. Semantics mattered less than dinner.

An hour later, the buck was butchered and out of sight when Bill Neish, the district Park Warden rode into camp. Bill was on his fall boundary patrol, intended to ensure that hunters contained their sport to the west of the Park Boundry. His attention was likely drawn to a single gunshot that sure seemed to come from within his territory.

Seeing that it was Tex, Bill relaxed. They were, after all, good friends in Banff, and Tex a respected member of the community. Soon the coffee pot was on, and steaming mugs poured around the fire.

"A shot? No I didn't hear anything around here," Tex replied to Bill's query. "We haven't seen a damn thing around here. Getting a little hungry, but of course we wouldn't touch anything in the Park."

Bill knew BS when he heard it.

"You know Tex, I've got a bottle of whisky back at my camp. It would go down pretty well right now, but it would go a hell of a lot better with some venison."

Tex wasn't about to bite that easily, but nor was Bill to be deterred. Several times the conversation bounced right back to Bill's bottle of hootch, and

Source: Tex Vernon-Wood

how good it would be with a little venison. Finally Tex figured that about then dinner was more important to Bill than law enforcement.

"Goddamn, Bill, this had better not be one of your tricks. Get your damn bottle and I'll get cooking."

As the bottle emptied, and the venison sizzled, the exact location of Wheeler's monument in relation to this particular deer's last breath lost all importance!

TEX

YOUNG ENGLISHMEN, arriving to work on the ranches of Alberta early in the 20th century, had more than their share of adapting to do. Their dandified dress, gentrified manners, and plummy accents all worked against them. Young Vernon-Wood had a lot more than most to shake. His name. God, it couldn't have been worse. Not only did he have the curse of a double barreled, hyphenated-up last name, his given name was a true curse.

Nello.

Sounded like Nelly, shortened to Nell, and was hell for an aspiring cowboy on this last frontier. After all, men were men, and some sissified version of a girl's moniker was not going to work. It was not a subject that Grandad was particularly fond of talking about, and has become the stuff of conjecture or family legend. There are two credible stories as to how Nello became Tex.

The simplest has it that when Nello applied for his first job on a ranch, not far from Medicine Hat, the foreman allowed as how there might be a cowboy's job open. "What's your name?"

There was a silence as the erstwhile range rider considered his future.

"Tex," he said, "my friends call me Tex."

An alternative version was passed on to me by Tex's son, Bill Vernon-Wood, and has more currency with me.

When upper-class young Englishmen hit Alberta, resplendent in tweeds and bowlers, they stuck out like sore thumbs. In an environment where some employers posted signs reading, "Englishmen Need Not Apply," those who needed work knew that they'd best blend in, fast.

Most hied themselves down to the Western Wear shop, where, badly advised by avaricious merchants, they decked themselves out in outlandish garb, more London stage than foothills sage. They paraded up and down the streets of Calgary, Lethbridge, and Medicine Hat in their frontier garb, true "Drugstore Cowboys."

Nello was no dandy, but working on a ranch near Medicine Hat, he badly needed a pair of chaps—the leather leggings that save a cowboys legs from being shredded in the bush or against barbed wire fences—which were an essential piece of ranch equipment. He bought a pair of the latest, greatest in protective fashion, known as "Texas Chaps." Back at the ranch, Nello was quickly nicknamed "Texas," which just as fast was abreviated to Tex. "Nello" was seldom, if ever, heard again!

To Simpson Pass with Bill Peyto

In March one year, Tex headed up to Simpson Pass with Bill Peyto, the legendary Banff packer, who had a trapline and cabin on the pass. The trip up Healey Creek was arduous, and Tex, the younger of the two, arrived at the cabin some time ahead of Peyto.

Simpson Pass is deep snow country, and trapper's cabins were built with a trap door on the roof to afford winter access. Tex set to work clearing the snow off the roof, and had the trapdoor open, set to jump down into the cabin, when Peyto came steaming into the clearing.

"Tex, stop!" He yelled. "Don't do that!"

Puzzled, Tex waited while Peyto rummaged around beside the cabin for a chunk of firewood. He carried it onto the roof and very deliberately held it over the open trap door. When the wood dropped into the dark cabin, it hit with a loud metallic clang, the sound of a very large bear trap slamming shut.

Tex peered down into the gloom of the cabin, and saw the firewood gripped in the jaws of the largest leghold trap around, right where he was about to land.

"Jesus, Bill, what did you put that there for?"

Peyto grunted. "Goddamned Harrison, he's been coming up here and stealing my grub. Figured that would slow him down some!"

APPENDIX B

A Gift from
Grandad Vernon-Wood

———————— • ————————

Recounted by his grandson, Harry W. Gow

I HAD FOR SOME TIME wanted to go to McGill University and at the same time improve my French-language skills, so while my move to Montréal at age 17 was what I wanted, it was a long way from my home base in Eastern British Columbia. I was therefore glad to get a compact package from Windermere in the mail; it had the heft and dimensions of a book. Opening it, I found a note from Tex. In it, he thanked me for the gift of a model river steamer I had sent him, described a local event, photos of which were included, and presented his gift book.

Tex wrote that reading the book, a National Geographic Society research publication of the 1920s Hacienda and Latifundia in Chile would give me to understand all there was to know about the functioning of Chilean society. I did so in the following months, and learned about the very subservient condition of the rural population of the country. I learned that there was "a great gulf fixed" between the wealthy landowners and the rural farm workers and peasants. I understood the lesson Tex wanted me to learn, that social inequalities were real and determined the fate of millions of people in the Americas.

When I was staying with him and Joan in the summer of 1946, I had mentioned something about what I thought was Canada's colonial status vis-à-vis the United Kingdom. The war had meant a growing together of the two countries, and the common war effort had meant some apparent sacrifice of sovereignty, something that was apparent even to a seven-year-old. Tex shot back that Canada was an independent country, and that Canadians did not have to ask Great Britain for permission to do anything! This surprised me, but I remembered this lesson in constitutional law from someone I had thought of as an unrepentant Englishman. I later had confirmation of his views when I found out that he had a subscription to what was then the *Manchester Guardian* (now *The Guardian*), the British left-liberal newspaper.

4 February, 2003

INDEX